INTERNET
MARKETING DEFINED

INTERNET MARKETING DEFINED

YOUR COMPLETE BLUEPRINT TO CREATING A SUCCESSFUL ONLINE BUSINESS

Richard McKelvey & Martin Saposnick

ISBN: 1522712666
ISBN 13: 9781522712664

PREFACE

SOLUTIONS ARE REVEALED "INSIDE THE BOX"

Internet Marketing Defined will teach you how to effectively build your business by using the tools of the internet. It presents a realistic and organized introduction to a complex "not-so-new" technology that is ever changing, that now has become "mainstream", and accepted as necessary for effective marketing campaigns.

> "This 'telephone' has too many shortcomings to be seriously considered as a means of communication. The device is inherently of no value to us." (Western Union memo, 1876.)

It's time to use "new" technologies and tools to look for information. Use of the internet is now the accepted practical way to get the result you're looking for, whether you are looking for the nearest Chinese restaurant, to attract new customers, speak with your grandchildren, to find a solution to a problem, share information with others, or find almost anything. It's time for you, the business owner, to join nearly 3 billion others worldwide who turn to the internet for the answers they need.

I am pleased to join with Rich McKelvey, "Chief Explainer", who reveals how to use the tools now available to get information from the internet, as our book explains how to market your product or service.

Information from our "Thinking Inside the Box" series will:

    show how to be seen by your prospective customers
    provide helpful information to existing customers
    introduce you to the tools that helps you analyze your website

The resources disclosed in the Boxes listed in the Content sections will show how to get the most use from the internet, to better position you with search engines, to communicate on social networks, to find customers, and to exchange thoughts with business associates, friends, and family.

The Inside the Box series will introduce and fine tune the tools and methods that will make your journey productive and maybe even fun. New doors will open that will help you understand the internet world as an introduction to the many necessary and some simply useful resources.

Martin I. Saposnick, Digital Architect

Summary of the Boxes

Box 1 - Foundation - Building a business and enhancing your brand with an internet presence. Page 1

Box 2 - World of Synchronicity -"Maximum Success is Achieved in Steps, "an introduction to the steps necessary to grow from novice to pro. Page 4

Box 3 - Learning from Observations, Learn from the best -An introduction to some of the most successful internet marketers.... see how it's done! Page 8

Box 4 - 12 Step Social Media Blueprint -How to implement a tactical approach to being visible. Page 11

Box 5 - Social Media 101, Intention & Focus - What is "Social Media" and how to achieve your desired results. Page 15

Box 6 - Social Media 102, Performance Management - How to get followers on twitter, gain friends on Facebook, build a LinkedIn presence, and realize the benefits of a YouTube presence...plus about 30 other social networks. Page 20

BOX 1

THE FOUNDATION

Building a business, whether it is on the internet or is a brick and mortar shop, requires almost the same set of strategies and skills.

You must determine at the onset which type of internet marketing campaign you wish to engage in.

Direct Marketing
Article Marketing
Affiliate Marketing
MLM (Multi-Level Marketing)
Network Marketing
Content Syndication
Direct Product Marketing

You can choose more than one. However, they must be compatible for you to identify a **carefully defined** market niche.

First, you need to select your mastermind team. (We'll talk about how helpful your team will be in a later Box.)

Selection of team members needs to be determined by the ability of each segment of the market you are going to engage. A team member need not be an expert in a chosen segment but MUST have the ability and the desire to become an expert.

Get a clear and focused idea of what your product will be. Design your website or blog to reflect the keywords most closely associated with your product.

Set up an accountability process and a timeline for completion.

Establish your internet brand (yourself or product) well in advance of ever attempting a product launch. This means to establish your accounts on all social media platforms asap.

Facebook
Twitter
LinkedIn
YouTube
Pinterest
Google+

Plus, a dozen more niche internet social sites.

Always keep in mind that any social site is never intended for selling. The sole purpose is to make contacts and to keep your name in front of your audience.

However, *every* action you take on social networks should be a part of your larger social media marketing plan.

That means every interaction you create, in Tweets, and comments and replies, and posts should all be guided by a plan and working toward the goals you have envisioned.

Creating a comprehensive social media marketing plan (SMMP) is one of the keys necessary for success.

You will find a complete SMMP in future boxes that make it easy for you to implement. Now, Box 1 may seem simplistic. It is not. If you do not set up your systems for operating a business in a cohesive, branded, and thoughtful way, you will not succeed, period.

This box is your call to action; it is now time to start a checklist and develop your plan. All the resources you will ever need, and most of them **free**, will be outlined in the next 39 boxes in a step by step explanation.

BOX 2

WORLD OF SYNCHRONICITY

"Maximum Success is Achieved in Steps"

N ow that you've had time to examine and think about the process in Box 1, we'll move to the next step in the building process.

Before we continue, you have to understand several important points:

The building blocks you'll need to make your marketing plans systemic are going to seem overwhelming at first. Don't let that concern you in the early stages. Everything will be explained on a concise step by step basis.

During your evolution from novice to pro, you will be inundated with offers of every system, super system, and super-secret system to come down the Turnpike in the last 10 years. Most of these so called systems that promise you untold fortunes are just plain junk, but a lot of the marketing ads designed to part you with your money are nothing short of genius.

There are no magic bullets. All of the information that is being sold is available to you, free of charge; you just have to be willing to extend the effort to seek it out. We will guide you every step of the way to gather all this information.

Remember, at all times, that your goal is building a long term, sustainable business that will generate you an income in proportion to the effort you put in. That being said, the soapbox is closed.

Take Action! ...

The first thing you will need to do is set up a spreadsheet. This is imperative in organizing your systems. Enter all of your website names, your user-names, and your passwords. A simple XL spreadsheet works fine for this purpose. If your computer doesn't come with one installed, you can buy one on eBay for about 5 dollars.

You will be databasing between 100 and 200 websites, so this is really essential.

Time now to decide if you wish to do website marketing or blogsite marketing/ Each one is equally effective; it is a personal preference. However, with blog marketing you don't have to contend with webmasters, hosting, etc. Either way, DO NOT use the free web sites that are offered through affiliate programs. You lose too much control.

If you decide to go with a website, you can download the CMS (Content Management System) at Wordpress.org, free of charge, and use it to design and build your own websites and capture pages. If you have never done this before, send us an email and we will send you a blueprint download to walk you through the entire process, step by step. You get it free of charge. (This is usually sold on the IM (Internet Market) for$19.95). Even if you have few computer skills, you can have a fully functional website published on the internet in about 6-8 hours.

If you decide to have someone design and build one for you, you will get a list of sites to go to in the resource box at Internet Visions Defined. The cost to outsource is usually just under $500.00.

Register your domain name with a hosting company. The usual cost is between $5.00 and $20.00 a year. There are many to choose from. We use Intuit.com, but GoDaddy.com and Hostgator.com are just as good. Do not purchase any upgrades or widgets. These are all available for free, and we will have a list for you in the resource box.

Give your domain name a considerable amount of thought. Do not make it to specific to any one product or market, because as you evolve, your current ideas on Internet Marketing will change dramatically.

Next you will want to set up your blog. This easiest place to do this is on Wordpress.org. It is free and the site box, where you establish a theme, has excellent tutorials for the beginner. Later on, as you progress in your branding, you will find out in the resource blog. This will be important as you define and refine your marketing campaign. Also, you will be walked through the process of getting your blog Indexed on Yahoo and MSN search engines instantly. Steer clear of Directories; in 2014 Google started imposing penalties on websites using directories.

Search engines will prove to be a virtual goldmine in back-links to your SEO process.

Now, as discussed in Box 1, you should establish your accounts in the top 6 Internet Social Sites, Facebook, Twitter, Google +, YouTube, Pinterest and LinkedIn. It is not important to fully understand the uses for these social sites, as this will all be explained in later boxes, as you go through the Synchronicity process. You NEED to use the same user-name and passwords for all your social networks, do not attempt to be cute with acronyms or dual meaning screen names. Keep your eye on the prize; you are building relationships here. In relationship marketing the first building block is Trust. Relationship Marketing will be discussed in detail in another box.

O.K., now you have work to do now, as outlined above. Stop getting ready to get ready, and get going. We are burning daylight here.

See you all in Box 3.

BOX 3

"Reference Content"

Learning from Observation

Welcome Back. At this point you should have set up your social media accounts, completed a little work on the Wordpress.org download, and registered your domain name.

Now what?

Always a big question when you come to this point. Many of you have been struggling with what type of IM business you wish to establish. Your initial ideas of bringing a single or group of products to the internet may now be taking on a different form.

.

When you started to work on the draft of your website, you were likely haunted by the question "What am I going to sell or produce that will make me money?" This is the most common problem facing "newbies" today. What should have taken you a day, is now taking you a week. You are not certain what to put in your website, or where to put it, and what kind of message you want to relay to your prospective clients.

This is where our "Reference Content" box comes into the picture.

Below you will find a list of some of the most successful internet business marketers, across many different product areas. Their internet addresses are included as links. (On your keyboard hit Ctrl and left click your mouse to view each website, or just copy and paste them in your address bar). This will save you hours of Google searching.

Go to as many, if not all, of these successful sites, and Observe and Learn. However, don't "opt in" to any of these sites, because you will find your email box overwhelmed with offers and solicitations. If you do feel a need to opt-in, then we recommend setting up a free e-mail account at Gmail, and sending all marketing mail there. This way, you'll be able to observe how their sales process continues without cluttering your main inbox. Keep in mind, however, that the sales process is generic, and will be fully laid out for you in a future Box.

Get a notepad, go to these sites, and jot down the ideas that you like or dislike. Observe their use of font colors, video insertions, calls to action, and what "free" gifts they are giving you to induce you to give them your email address. Get the "feel" for the site. You are here to learn, so write down the ideas you may want to include on your site. Find the "commonality" that all these marketers are using. Ask yourself "what is their main goal? "and "how have they appealed to me?" Then ask yourself if you would buy from these marketers, and why would you do so. Ask yourself if you trust these people.

Remember, you are learning and exploring, and you have to dig into the operation that you are observing in order to learn. Some of these sites are well crafted, some downright sleazy, some cunning, and some run of the mill, but each serves a purpose. Keep in mind that each of these marketers have been in business and making money for 10+ years. Learn from them. We installed these as hyperlinks so you can click on them.

www.earlytorise.com
www.daniellevis.com
www.hyperresponsivemarketingsecrets.com
www.thegaryhalbertletter.com
www.dankennedy.com
www.mattfurey.com
www.michaelcage.com
www.imnewswatch.com
www.davedee.com
www.tradethemarkets.com

Now, these 11 sites should give you plenty of ideas and get your thought processes working. Notice that we have not included any "dog and pony show" internet marketers, of the world. They are not the models you want to follow; as most intelligent online shoppers would not give you a second look.

So folks, stop getting ready to get ready, let's get to work. We are burning daylight! Next, in Box 4, you'll receive the complete 12 step "Social Media Blueprint" that took a year to perfect. It is very exciting; this step by step blueprinting to get you exposure will truly amaze and inspire you.

'Till then, think only success. Rich and Marty.

BOX 4

12 STEP SOCIAL MEDIA BLUEPRINT

This is the first of 5 Blueprints you will be receiving. It is important for you to follow each Blueprint and engage its content and structure. All 5 Blueprints are the basis of your success in total Internet Business Marketing.

Get involved– Be Social, be Real. If you want to drive traffic from Social Media Sites you are going to need to get involved. You will always need to keep in mind that direct advertising and promotions rarely work on Social Media. You need to <u>contribute</u> and provide great content (or links and references to it) for you to benefit. It is more of a marathon approach, but one that will certainly pay off for you. Start by listing as many Social Media communities and other "Social" areas you can find in your market (Your Target Market).

Create a Facebook account (www.facebook.com). Facebook is by far the best Social Network to use for your business. Almost daily, they come out with new applications to help you in business. (In Box 8, we teach you how to refine your Facebook ads to target your micro-market with laser precision). Customize your account and invite all your existing customers and prospects to send you a friend request on Facebook. Before you know it you'll start to experience the Viral

Benefits of Social Networking, and you will be connecting to new prospects almost daily.

Create a Twitter account (www.twitter.com). Twitter has quickly become a valuable communications tool. The main purpose of using Twitter is to communicate with others in your market. It is also a great way to automatically syndicate links each time you post important content.

Create an Instagram account (www.instagram.com) and a Flickr.com account (www.flickr.com). These are both great online photo hosting services. Almost all of the most popular Social Media services interact with Flickr and Instagram. You can upload a single photo to Flickr/ Instagram and have it automatically published in a large number of different areas across the world wide web.

Always remember: Photos get many more click views and a huge response rate in relation to any other form of communication text. So use Flickr/Instagram to share photos of your personal life and things related to your business. People are magnetically drawn to photographs.

Create an account on Quora (https://www.quora.com). The blogging feature that they added in 2014 is a rich source of backlinks and for going viral through your followers.

Create a LinkedIn account (www.linkedIn.com). LinkedIn is far and above the best Social Network for professionals. You can attract new customers as well as potential partners by using LinkedIn. It is always a good Network to start establishing yourself as an expert in the field of your business.

Install the Twitter App in Facebook. This auto-syndicates any posts you make on Twitter to your Facebook profile page.

Install the Flickr App in Facebook. This auto-syndicates all photos that you add to Flickr to your Facebook profile page.

Set up your Facebook page's "Notes" section with your Blog RSS Feed. This auto-syndicates any posts you write on your Blog to your Facebook profile page. In addition, install the RSS Feed App for your Facebook account. This syndicates your Blog posts TWICE giving you more exposure.

Post Comments on Other Blogs. Find as many blogs as you can in your target market, get involved in the "conversation" by posting in the comment sections. <u>DO NOT</u> promote your URL in your comments. Your URL will be linked from your name when you submit the comment post form. Make sure and be careful to only post comments that provide solid value to the conversation. You want to post your comments in a conversational form, but be firm in the tone… you are the expert.

Create accounts on The Top Social News Sites. Join and participate in News sites like (www.digg.com), and (www.reddit.com). Remember: 95% of the time you should submit and vote on other related resources and sites. It's important to vote on relevant resources. (on your own site about 5% of the time).

Only submit your own pages when you have something really valuable to share. Don't submit every piece of content you create. Always keep your activity as "natural" as possible. This is certainly another <u>Observe and Learn</u> process like you studied in Box 3.

Create Accounts on the Top Social Bookmarking Sites. Join (www. Delicious.com). And (www.Stumbleupon.com). Again, remember: Bookmark related resources and sites, but for the most part not on your own site. Keep your activities natural here also.

Well, you now have the complete 12 Step Social Media Blueprint. It is not the end; it is the beginning. At this point, even if you are not quite sure how these sites will work for you, go ahead and establish yourself. Everything will become crystal clear as we progress through the 40 Box process. Remember to keep your spreadsheet out for your names and passwords, etc. We like to use www.Lastpass.com to keep organized. You can read about spreadsheets and programs like LastPass in the addendum section of our website.(www.internetmarketingdefined.com)

In Box 5, you will be walked through all the applications of the Social Media Sites, be given links to automate most processes, and get a ton of shortcuts to make the direction you are headed in easier to attain.

We will also be starting our Blog and Article processes with all the links and sites you'll need to syndicate yourself throughout the Internet Marketing World. It is our goal to make sure that you are seen everywhere.

OK. Now you have work to do. Stop getting ready to get ready. We are burning daylight here.

BOX 5

Social Media

Intention and Focus

N ow that you have completed your set up work in Box 4, we are going to delve into the how and why.

Many of the social media participants today think they have found the perfect vehicle to sell their products and wares. They soon become disillusioned. They haven't a clue as to why their efforts aren't producing results. It is simple once you learn the true meaning of "Social Media."

People come to and engage in social media because they want to be informed, educated, amused, and appreciated. The third greatest need in human beings, behind food and shelter, is the need to be accepted. This need is not met when you, as a social person, are being sold something. It does not matter that the product or service you provide is the best and greatest; it still falls far short of what everyone is looking for in social media.

The sole intention for social media in your business is to _**introduce**_ yourself. Letting the social world know who _**you**_ are. Let them know that you are a real person, and that you wish to interact with them. It has to be real on your part. You cannot fake it; people will pick up on it and leave you in a New York minute.

You _**must**_ participate with the sole intention of providing value to those you inter-react with, without expectation of a return. Do this, and your marketing efforts down the road will be successful. Remember, this is a marathon, not a hundred-yard dash.

Once you establish yourself through non-marketing efforts, people will seek you out, to learn what you do, and why and how you do it. They will have built a trust relationship, and if you have something that is of value to them, they become willing and able clients.

You will not have to sell them anything, they will "want" to buy from you, because you have become a reliable and trusted source.

Now, let's get into the mechanics a little bit.

Once your 12 steps are in place, you want to build and link them. This step progresses in direct proportion to the effort you put into it. Keep in mind, at this point, you still do not have a website. It is not important now; it will become **very important** later on.

Let's start with Twitter. Go to www.tweepi.com and set up account(s) to manage your followers and following lists. It's a free service. Start by generating about 250 people to follow. 250 is a good rule of thumb and will return to you about 50 followers (20%). Do every other day for 4 followings of 250 each on all of your accounts. (This number allows you to stay under the radar for Twitter to recognize the automatic robot). Note: Twitter will suspend your account if they feel you are using a robot to gather followers/following. At this point you should create up to four accounts, but no more (refer to the Box 5 addendum on our website to learn what to name the accounts).

While you are gathering people to follow, post tweets on your accounts. Keep it real and keep it interesting. Just a comment on a current event will suffice. As you gather people to follow, those that follow you back may also send you a DM (direct message). Most of these will be sent by auto responders. You will know these because they always contain a link to their sales page. These replies you can and should ignore and delete.

Look for replies that a real person actually sent to you. These DM's should be replied to in a timely manner. After you reply, look at their list of followers/following and select some of the profiles that you find interesting. Re-tweeting posts that you like is also an excellent way to pick up followers, as people are flattered when you do this and are very likely to follow you in return.

At this point, you will start to get an idea of the areas of interest of the people that you want to follow and of those whom you want to follow you. Keep it a little broad for now, and you can make a narrower focus later on. You'll likely change your ideas on the exact market you wish to approach as your knowledge of what the marketplace is seeking evolves.

The most natural starting point for you should come from something you are passionate about. It could be your hobby or an area of expertise that you are familiar with. This is the beginning of the first of the four formulas you will use in Social Media:

Passion + Interest + A Big Market + Data Research Tools = Your Niche Market.
But let us not get lost in the details at this point. These four important formulas will be explained in detail in a later box.

Now it is time to start linking your accounts. Go to www.hootsuite. com and open an account. You can link up to 4 Twitter accounts here. Also include your Facebook account and Google+ account.

Next, write a short article about your passion, and keep it between 300 and 500 words. Publish your article on hubpages.com. Make sure you always shorten the links to your article using a bit.ly or tinyurl. com, and use the shortened link whenever you post on all your social media accounts.

Note: Make it a habit to copy and paste of all your article bit.ly's to a notebook you have set up for this purpose. This way, when you write a tweet on a random thought, you can simply open your notebook and copy and paste the link to the article whenever you see an opportunity. A very interesting thing happens here. Google searches and adds links to articles from Twitter. So, use a keyword rich Tweet with your bit.ly attached, and Google will PageRank you (trust us, you want this).

For example: if you were to write an article on teaching a parrot how to talk…

Send a Tweet saying, "#I am teaching my parrot to talk" or "#Talking parrots made fun" or "#Training my parrot to talk", (you get the idea) with your bit.ly attached. Now when anyone in the world Google's those words; they will be directed to your article. And of course, to get traffic, your article will have your web address attached.

Note: The # symbol, called a hashtag, is used to mark keywords or topics in a Tweet. The hashtag symbol # before a relevant keyword or phrase (no spaces) in a Tweet is used to categorize Tweets and help them show up in Twitter Search.

By this process of linking, you are starting the internet marketing sales process.

Now, we do not want you to get ahead of yourself. Remember in Box 4, step 1, you were told that this is a marathon and not a sprint. Don't go running off to www.articles.com and think that you will get the same results. That is a whole different venue and will be explained in a later box. www.tumblr.com, is the perfect platform for a beginner.

On the other side, go to your Facebook account and activate the Twitter app. When you do this, all the Tweets that you post on Twitter, will automatically appear on your Facebook page. With this in mind, keep your Twitter posts focused on introducing yourself to the world. All your friends on Facebook will see them too.

After a day or two set up a Tumblr account and link it to your Twitter and Facebook accounts. This may also be a good time to establish a separate Facebook account that you will use just for business and social marketing.

Do not be concerned that you do not have a lot of followers on Twitter or a lot of friends on Facebook. In Box 6, we devote a ton of time, taking you through the process, step by step on building and developing followers and friends, and on how to segment them to bring maximum results.

Also in Box 6, we show you how to link ALL the social sites into one aggregate, so you can control them all from one location.

OK, folks, you have work to do. Stop getting ready to get ready. We are burning daylight here.

Rich and Marty.

BOX 6

SOCIAL MEDIA

Performance Management

Let's now walk through the steps for building your Twitter, Facebook, Myspace, and LinkedIn account lists, etc.

Your main purpose at this stage is to acquire both targeted followers and targets account to follow for all your social media accounts. We'll start by doing it the old fashioned way. We will cover using automated services in a later Box. For now, let's do it manually, in order to get a feel for segmenting the market.

Imagine that you just opened a brand new Twitter account, and you call yourself "Parrot Coach".

Step 1: At the top of your **Twitter** page find the bar that says "Home, Moments, Notifications, Messages."

Step 2: Enter the word Parrot in the search box. In the upper right corner there will be a box with a few suggestions from your market niche. Click on "view all". Wow…pretty amazing, isn't it? You have just accessed a very large number profiles of people who have the word Parrot, either in their name or their bio.

Step 3 Now, enter the word Parrot in the search box.

Step 4: Scroll down the list and click on the "Follow icon" that is next to their name, for each profile that you find interesting. Keep your follow requests just below 250 profiles to start. This is about the maximum number of follow requests you can make in a day in order to look natural. That is about all you can do on the first day.

Step 5: On the second day, when you open your newly established account, you will see that you have gained some followers, and this is natural to the process. Repeat the same request process that you did on the first day.

Step 6: After you have made your day 2 requests, you'll need to send out a tweet that is related to your passion about training parrots. Keep it simple and informative, always tweet in the same way that you would hold a normal conversation. After all, you ARE a real person. (Now, here is some inside information:

As people have followed you back, you now have access to all the people that follow them, and to all the people that they follow. Click on their icon and their page will appear. On the upper right hand side of the page, underneath their Twitter name and icon, you will find their following and followers numbers. Click on the people they are following, because they will follow people that are, in some shape or form, also related to their interests. (in this case, Parrots.)

Step 7: Let's expand this by using our Twitter followers to build our Facebook friends. Using a separate tab or window in your browser, go ahead and log into your Facebook account. Preferably, your Facebook page is following the same theme as your target audience. For instance, on Facebook, you should have chosen something like Parrot Coach or Parrot Trainer, etc.

Step 8: Go back to your Twitter tab. Scroll down the "Following" list that you previously opened. A lot of people on this list will post something like.... "If you enjoy my Tweets, connect with me on Facebook", and they will include their Facebook link. BINGO. This is exactly what you are looking for. Click on that link and it will re-direct you to that person on Facebook. Click on the friend request. Since the request came from the Twitter link you will get an auto-matic acceptance.

Step 9: Here is where a pretty cool thing happens. Facebook is pro-grammed to build friends exponentially. You will now start to receive "friend suggestions" on your Facebook page. Click on these and new friend requests will go out. It is by the very nature of Facebook, that almost everyone that receives this type of request will accept them. However, there is one caveat, DO NOT send out more than 12 re-quests in a 24-hour period. More than 12 may trigger a spammer alert on Facebook, and they will close your account. Do this slowly, make a few requests, then read some comments, make a post or whatever, then go back to the requests. This makes it seem all the more natural to the Facebook search engine.

Now, at the same time you are building your Twitter presence, you are also building your Facebook presence.

Keep in mind, while you are doing this, to post comments on your Facebook page to show your "friends" that you are a real person. Also on Twitter, if you read an interesting post re-tweet it. This is consid-ered a compliment on Twitter, and helps gain you followers.

Tip: Put the Twitter App and the Facebook App on your BlackBerry, iPhone, or any smartphone, and this way you can send tweets or post comments whenever you have some idle time. The more active you are; the more positive responses you will receive.

Step 10: You need to repeat this process on Myspace. Many people consider Myspace passé. However, they have over 200 million active users, and this number is nothing to sneeze at. If you don't have a Myspace account, go sign up. They have hundreds of really cool apps, and their mobile connection is second to none. As you will learn in Box9, the mobile connection is going to become very important to you.

Step 11: You can also do your YouTube links directly into your Facebook and Myspace accounts directly from the info box. YouTube allows you to annotate videos with your Facebook and Myspace links. This will translate into significant inbound traffic to your fan pages.

Note: At this point of the process you may not already have a YouTube presence, but that will change in Box9.

Just be aware of this. YouTube will very likely surpass Google as the leading search engine in the near future, which makes linking these accounts together all the more important.

Step 12: LinkedIn...In our opinion, this is the best social media site for open forum discussions. Participating in these forums allows you to capture a ton of backlinks to your website. If you cannot find a Featured Discussion on LinkedIn that addresses your target audience, that is great, because it gives you the opportunity to start one. Better yet, if there is no LinkedIn group for your industry, you can start that also.

So, go ahead and link your Facebook page on your LinkedIn profile. The best place to do this is in the description of your current position; put a hyperlink to your fan page at the bottom of the description.

At this point of the learning curve, that's enough for now. We don't want to start losing you in the details. Of which, there are many. So far, we've touched on the top Social Media sites. There are over 30 sites that we believe cannot be ignored, including Flicker, Picassa, Vimeo, Tumbler, Xanga, etc. But do not worry, we will get to them all.

In Box7 we will go through the process of starting and setting up your Blogs and Articles. Most importantly, we will show you how to publish them and connect all of your Blogs and Articles to all your Social Media sites. You'll see how everything comes full circle.

In Box7, we'll show you an amazing trick that will push your Blog or Article to the first page of Google within 1 hour of publishing it. This is incredible since it normally takes up to one week for any Blog or Article just to get *indexed*, before Google even looks at it.

OK Folks, you have work to do. Stop getting ready to get ready. We are burning daylight here.

Rich & Marty

BOX 7

BLOGS AND ARTICLES

One of the most misunderstood areas of Internet Business is understanding the difference between a Blog and an Article.

Believe it or not many blog and article writers themselves do not know the difference between the two.

Let's clear this up…

Article: This is **a writing of expertise**. An article is the longer (500 words or more) of the two types. When you hear the word "Article," immediately replace it in your mind with the words "News Article. "An article is a publishing (writing) that is totally objective on a subject. It is verified with facts and statistics, and filled with credible back up information and references that support the article. An article leads the reader to a conclusion.

Blog: This is a **writing of passion**. A blog is the shorter of the two types. It can be one sentence, or a video, or a handful of paragraphs. Generally, blogs are 250 to 350 words. A blog is the opinion of the writer and does not need to be supported by facts or research. It is generally written about what the blogger finds interesting or loves to do. The blogger is sharing his *passion* with you and inviting you to comment on it.

Hopefully that clears up any confusion between a Blog and an Article for you.

Another factor that needs to be clear is that both Blogs and Articles have identical missions for us. Each is meant to direct and drive traffic (people) to our website. Once they get to our website, we can convert them into clients and customers.

We suggest that you start simply:

Use *www.blogger.com* for your blogs. Using the Google+ profile that you created gives you an identity on Google properties and connects you with your readers, allowing them to share and recommend your content on the web and on Google+.

Use *www.ezinearticles.com* for your articles. There are many opinions for the hosted and non-hosted platforms for the blogs and articles, but for now follow the KISS formula. (Keep It Simple......)

Here are the essentials that you must have on your blogs and articles:

A Contact Button
A Capture Box
A Comment Box
Keyword Tags
Plug-ins
A Theme
And, of course, a LINK to your website
A Defined Niche

It may look strange that "A Defined Niche" is placed as the last entry on the list. We placed it there so that it will be the freshest in your mind.

If you do not put a solid plan in place as to whom you are blogging to, your writing will be all over the road. Take your time, identify your target market (people), and engage yourself in your passion. This is something you can't fake...nor should you want to. If you are not blogging about something that you have a true passion about, you will lose focus, energy, and the will to continue. Start a blog for the fun of it, not for the hope of earning from it. If you do the fun thing, the money will follow later on.

Would you like to see exactly where you will receive the money from? Here is the most important ingredient in your blog or article

Consistency

Once you start your blog or article campaign, don't just post 5-6 posts in a week and then leave it dry for a month. You need to do your blog writing on a schedule. Two to three times a week, every third day, once a week, whatever! Whatever frequency you choose, **keep it regular and consistent**.

Google ranks blogs according to your activity. We've included an addendum on our site that outlines our recommended Social Media Calendar, and how to set your goals on it.

Activity brings incoming links, and incoming links bring a higher Google ranking. People follow this. (In a later box, you will learn about Blogrolls and Blog Directories).

The next most important thing in your Blog or Article is your opening line. This is the first line that follows your title. Research shows that you have about 5 seconds before the average reader hits the "back" button, so this line MUST capture their attention. It MUST engage them. So, spend more time on creating your opening line than you do on the whole first paragraph.

Learn to craft. Learn the tricks of professional copywriters. For instance, the most commonly used trick is to ask a question that the reader can only answer with a "yes".

Example; YOU READ IT IN THE SECOND SENTENCE ABOVE THE WORD CONSISTENCY (above)

Now it's time to give some thought as to why everyone says you NEED an RSS feed on your blog, and what does President Obama have to do with it?

Were you engaged you with that question?

OK, then, let's add some additional steps to take when setting up your blog or article accounts.

Step 1: Make sure that when you start a blog account, you add your RSS feed to your Yahoo and MSN accounts. You will get instant rankings on these search engine giants the moment someone links to your RSS feed in their search engine specific account.

Step 2: You can speed up the ranking by subscribing to your own blog on your MSN account through your Yahoo account, and your Yahoo account through your MSN account.

Note: The spiders don't make the connection that it is you subscribing to you. Pretty neat trick.

Step 3: The next natural step is to link your blog to your Social Media accounts. Put out a few Tweets to say "I just put up a new blog on teaching my Parrot how to talk. "Then send out a status update blast on Facebook letting your friends know about your Parrot Teaching blog. In other words, let all your contacts throughout social media know where to find your blog. This will translate into visitors and comments, and this is how to make your Blog and Articles go viral. Start a Facebook Fan Page on "Talking Parrots" and link it back to your blog. This will give you backlinks from Facebook to your blog. Google loves this kind of traffic.

In a later box, you will learn about using "Blog Contests" to give a big boost to your blog following.

One more important thought for today.

Don't lose focus on the fact that you are using Blogs and Articles as a part of the overall big picture plan.

Remember, these two tools serve the sole purpose of bringing traffic to your website...your "Money Spot."

They are tools, and nothing more than that. Down the road you'll outsource or delegate these tasks to one of your staff members to maintain. They do not become "You."

In the resource area in the addendum to Box 11, you will learn all the functions that will enable you to do this, with all the necessary links to fully automate this task. Do not become absorbed in this activity. Budget your time accordingly when you are doing your blogs and articles; there is plenty of other things you'll be doing with your time.

OK Folks, now you have work to do. Stop getting ready to get ready. We are burning daylight here.

Rich and Marty.

BOX 8

SEARCH ENGINE OPTIMIZATION PART 1

Well, now that we have put some pieces of the puzzle together in your Internet Marketing platform, we now want to see it get to the places where it can generate interest. That is done by optimizing your website so that the search engines will find it. (Much easier said than done).

Understand, that there is an entire industry built around SEO. Everyone is fighting for the high ground, which is being the first page listing on Google, Yahoo, and MSN search engines.

Since there are so many professional SEO companies, you have a tremendous amount of competition to get to the first page and then to stay on the first page. If you have a deep bankroll then you can skip Box 8, and hire an SEO firm to do the work for you.

If you go this route, plan to spend about $1000 initially and about $75.00 per month for site maintenance (and then hope for the best).

If that is not your case, we'll show you how to set up and maintain your SEO campaign. With some hard work, and devoted time, you can achieve the same results as any of the big-time SEO companies.

But always keep in mind that this training is intended to give you the big picture overview, so that you can systemize this operation and to delegate this task to an admin. This book's training series is focused on your "Freedom", and not on creating a ton of additional "mini-jobs" for you. So always keep the Ultimate Goal in focus (you making money without doing any work).

To start, we will be working on:

> Meta-Tags
> Title and Header Tags
> Keyword Proximity
> Sitemap Inclusion
> Anchor Text

Meta-Tags.

First of all, if you are like most internet business owners, you don't even know what a meta-tag is, or know what is it supposed to do.

So, how would you know that it is important?

A meta-tag (meta-data) is simply a set of instructions and identifiers that exist solely for search engine spiders to read and let them know what a web page is all about. It describes the content of the web page in spider language. Period. It has no other function.

This is not intended to teach you HTML code in order to infuse your website. It is intended to make you aware, as a business person, of what meta-tags look like and how they would describe your web page.

Nearly anyone who designs a web page just includes basic stock info, such as terms like "robot follow" then your URL by the way, URL means: Universal Resource Locator (we expand on this more in another box). Designers will likely add one or two keywords.

Here is what you want to see when you look at your own meta-tags:

```
<HEAD>
<TITLE> Parrot Talking Training World</TITLE>
<META name=" Description" Content= Everything you wanted to know about training your parrot to talk"
<META name= "keywords" Content "Parrot, Parrots, Parrots Training, Parrots Talking>
</Head>
```

This code is like what you want to see in your own meta-tags. It has some main keywords inserted. This is not to be confused with your keyword section, which we'll set up separately.

Now pay attention: Most web designers only put meta tags and keywords on the main page, and all the other page's link to the main page. (This is the lazy way of doing it). EACH page of your website MUST have its own meta-tags and keywords, because every page tells a different story. Whoever builds your site must be given the instruction to do this.

Title and Header Tags.

Most website builders call the title (index) page the same as the URL. Your Title Tag MUST always include your Primary Keyword Phrase. So, in place of www.parrotworld.com, your title tags should say "Parrot Training Talking." Again, the title tag must be put on every page.

Header Tags<head> are important because using head tags within the content of your web page highlights the important text on your page.

Sitemaps.

Here you will read a professional secret (and it's free) ... Go to http://www.XML-Sitemaps.com and follow the 4 easy steps. Select the frequency to update daily. Make sure your administrative assistant has this, and every time you update or add to the site have them go back here and recall the spiders into action.

After you create your sitemap, become a Google Webmaster (also for free) at www.google.com/webmasters/sitemaps/siteoverview.com; from here you can update and you will be able to see internet traffic statistics to your entire site.

Put this in your primary toolbox, it is very powerful.

Keyword proximity:

Don't be timid here; we always include our keywords in the very first sentence of our webpage content. Then add one more variant of the keyword before ending the first paragraph. Remember, the further down the page that your keywords appear, the less relevance that the search engine spiders place upon them. Add the keywords one more time in the second paragraph, and then you will be done. If you add more than 3 keyword phrases, it may appear that you are "stuffing" keywords in your content. Stuffing causes Google to actually downgrade your page ranking.

Anchor Text:

Anchor Text is really important in SEO. It allows you to describe a link, either internal or external. So rather than putting your website name in the anchor text, you will put your main keywords in the anchor text, and this allows you to rank in the search engines for "specific keywords" instead of just your URL.

Now that you are able to analyze the structure of your site SEO properties, you want to visit the sites of your competition within your niche. Take a look at their keywords and meta tags to get a feel for what yours should be. If they are successful sites, you can "borrow" some of the keywords and phrases. Evidently they work; otherwise the sites would not be ranked high.

This is in no way unethical or underhanded; it is a common practice for all webmasters to improve their own sites.

In the next Box, we will walk you through the process of building qualified backlinks to your website. This is the next step to getting the high SEO ranking that you are seeking. We will show you our "killer" back linking campaign, using Authority Blogs, Communities and Forums.

This is a time consuming process, but we have discovered 3 very potent websites that will accelerate your process tenfold. They will all be explained in the next box.

OK Folks, now you have work to do. Stop getting ready to get ready, we are burning daylight here.

Rich & Marty

BOX 9

Starting to close the Circle Backlinks

N ow we'll start the process to get your work noticed, appreciated, and most importantly, profitable.

So far, you have learned how to build your basic structures. If you've been doing your work, you are gaining ground in your Social Networking efforts. You have the tools to put your articles and blogs in place, and you have tuned up your website with the correct keywords and phrases.

Now what? Your website is published and it is just waiting for all the hordes of visitors to come rushing in. Well, if it seems that nobody is looking at your website besides yourself, you are probably pretty close to the mark.

Visitors do not come rushing in, they are pushed in. They get there because they typed in "Train my Parrot to talk" in the search engine and YOU popped up on the first page. This is the highest quality of visitors you can ever get, because they are viral. They came looking for you, and you showed them your address. You showed them where to find you.

You got to the first page because you had a lot of backlinks to your website. What exactly is a backlink you ask?!

A backlink is simply a vote.

It is a vote from other websites and blogs and articles.

The more votes you get, the more the search engines (Google, Yahoo, MSN) like you. The more that the search engines like you, the higher up the page rank ladder you go. Backlinks tell the search engines that your website is relevant and meaningful.

Get enough votes and you become President (of the internet).

This is why it is important to concentrate on your backlinks
.
This is done by visiting all the blogs and forums that are within your niche target market that you can possibly find. Then, post comments in the comment box including a link back to your website. The comments must be meaningful and add to the conversation. This is why this process is time consuming and can't be rushed.

Note: This is definitely a project you want to pass onto your admin as soon as you become proficient yourself and set up the guidelines that you want followed.

The first thing you must establish is that the website, blog, or forum has a "do follow" link. Otherwise, don't bother commenting, because you'll be wasting your time.

Note: A "do follow" is a site that allows you to leave a comment **AND** "post your URL website address in the comment box." (**otherwise there is no backlink**).

Be sure that you are linking to an **"Authority"** Blog or Forum or Website. Authority" sites are the ones that have standing and influence in the blogosphere. (Gee, don't we wish we invented that word...)

If you want to research whether a particular site is an Authority, you can find all the information on www.technorati.com, the leader in ranking blogs and sites.

However, here is one trick of the trade for you. (Actually, not many people in the trade know about it).

Use the Mozilla/Firefox browser, and type in:https://addons. mozilla.org/en-US/firefox/extensions/?sort=featured.

Now, on the second page of the collection that opens up, you will see a "free" add-on called NoDoFollow. (https://addons.mozilla.org/ en-US/firefox/addon/nodofollow/?src=ss)

Go ahead and download this add-on. You will find this to be the easiest application for finding out which blogs are "follow" or "non-follow" sites. This little trick will save you hours upon hours of searching.

We have a more advanced search tool that we will show you in a later box, down the road a bit. But you need to learn the nuts and bolts of this type of searching before you go advanced.
Now that you know a few tricks, back to basics.

Always remember to leave only meaningful comments on the sites so that the administrator retains your backlinks and does not just delete them. Also, this is a great way to build relationships with the site owners that may pay off for you down the road.

Also, when you are making your backlink, always use your Anchor Text. This requires a little HTML code for you to insert, but it is well worth the effort.

So, in our example, the link to enter looks like this:

<ahref=http://www.parrotworld.com>talking parrots</a>|

Insert your ↑ website and keyword phrase in the above when providing backlinks

By doing this, not only is your website backlinked, but you also get ranking for your specific keywords. Very, powerful stuff here folks. Learn it. Also, you will be in the top 1% of all the people that leave comments for backlinks. You have just learned how to go the "extra mile."

If you would like to do some quick back linking just to get a feel for things, just head on over to www.digg.com or www.slashdot.org or www.furl.net, and prowl the lists.

All of the blogs on these sites are "dofollow" sites and you can get some practice in and also start your back linking campaign.

OK, Folks. Now you have work to do. Stop getting ready to get ready. We are burning daylight here.

Rich and Marty

BOX 10

"THE CROSSROADS"

So... why is it that it's so hard to make it in the Internet Marketing world?

The best answer is that anyone with any online experience knows that task completion and getting things accomplished online are very difficult, especially when you are in learning mode by yourself.

So, Box 10 is labeled, the "Crossroads" because you have now come to this point. You know enough now that you should be able to make an informed decision on whether you want to continue on this endeavor.

The first nine Boxes were simply an overview in simplistic form. Box 10, of course is your own personal crossroads box, and box 11 is a resource box to help you with all the references you will need to be able to complete boxes 12 thru 24.

We call this program:

The "Twelve Pillars of Internet Success"

Each box of the Twelve Pillars is an in-depth explanation of the process. Detailed in linear fashion as the exact and correct way to establish your internet business, launch it, and keep it running and profitable.

In the pages ahead you will be getting the benefit of tons of knowledge that we already have, and provide, if you need it, support and guidance, along with any of the tools that you may need, but may not have, or be able to afford.

Most important is the accountability support we provide, that everyone needs sometimes in order to inspire themselves to get things done.

REALITY CHECK TIME:

It is widely accepted that 96% of the folks that attempt to start an internet business fail. The problem with this statistic is that no one explains WHY.

Here are a few reasons to share with you:

Confusion of which direction to go (Too many choices)

- *Information Overload (Very extreme in this industry)*
- *Confidence (Most have NEVER attempted business)*
- *And have no clue where to begin*
- *Skeptics (family, friends, etc...)*

Rich said, "The very first time I ever saw that statistic, (only 4 succeed) I said to myself out loud, as I chuckled, "Well, it looks like me and 3 other people are going to have a blast doing this thing. (Although I wasn't really concerned with the other 3)." But that is him, and this is about YOU.

We only want to stress this point to you because it is from here forward that the real work begins. This is the point where you either take a step back, or reconsider going to a mainstream job.

Or take the journey to the other side of Box 11 with us, and follow your own purpose. This should not be minimized; it is going to be a lot of work in the beginning, and internet marketing is by no means easy. The rewards, however, will be well worth the effort. We will give you the knowledge of the Web. Nothing else is guaranteed, because it is totally up to you what you do with it.

We will only promise one thing: we will stay with you throughout the entire journey. So, if you decide to stay and learn, here is a little idea of what you will see and learn on the other side of Box 11.

(just one of many diagrams and charts and graphs in the marketing learning process.)
In the diagram below which of the black dots is larger than the other. And why?? Take your time and look closely:

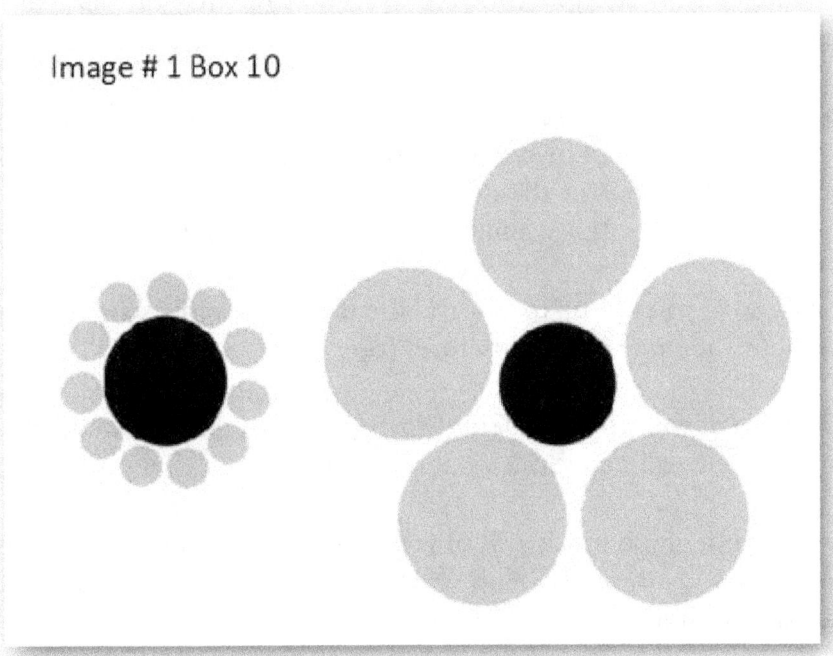

Image # 1 Box 10

If you picked the one on the left, you are wrong.

If you picked the one on the right, you are wrong.

The black dots that are displayed are exactly the same size. The only thing that is different is the perception of the customer.

The one on the left is a standalone product, with no ancillary benefits to you (consequently of lesser value to the client.)

The one on the right is your base product, surrounded by your up-sells, add-on's, and continuity income streams. (Of course the verbiage was removed in the circles).

This tutorial shows and fully explains how the revenue from the same product can be multiplied by 8 to 10 times of what the standalone product can generate.

So, you see, it is a simple, yet very powerful diagram as to how you present your product or service. It shows you how one dot (left one) is a sale and a goodbye, the other dot (right one) is a sale, and a sale, and a sale, and a sale. (We like the dot on the right better).

For those of you willing to go onto the other side of Box 10, the price is exactly the same as it was before, **<u>free.</u>**

For those of you who decide not to go to the other side, well, maybe someday you will figure out what the real cost was.

In any event, good luck to all of you, and, hey, if you're coming, let's stop getting ready to get ready. We have work to do, and we are burning daylight here.

Rich and Marty

BOX 11

R-E-S-O-U-R-C-E

First and foremost, you have to understand that a resource is a TOOL. It is not a magic bullet or a panacea to cure all problems. However, with the correct use of all the resources that you will be given in Boxes 12 thru 24, your problems will be few and far between.

By now, as outlined in Boxes 1 thru 10, you should have most of the fundamental infrastructure in place. All of your social media accounts should be set up, as you have you will still be branding yourself, and clients will buy from you and not XYZ company.

As an example, if you check all the SM (social media) sites for Rich, you will find out that his photo is the same.

You need to be a little more focused at this point on exactly what product or service you will be basing your internet business on.

When you decide on the product or niche that you wish to concentrate on, you want to make sure that your actual website URL is not product or niche "specific." So, if you are teaching parrots to talk, you will need to broaden your site name to something like

"PetTeaching.com". This way you can expand your product line as necessary, without creating a whole new site every time you create a new product.

Your website is a tool. It is not you, it is not your company. It is only ONE part of your resources.

However, it is what we like to call an Anchor resource. Anchor resources are the basis and the foundation of your business, and you will be getting several dozens of them.

Once your web-site is published on-line, go to www.statcounter.com and register for a free account. This is absolutely a great add-on tool," worth at least one or two hundred dollars to you. It is totally FREE, until the day you get over 9,000 page hits per day, when you are required to upgrade.

This is example of what we like to call a "tangible" tool. However, it is not an anchor resource. Understand that, as you grow your business, other tools will apply to increase your business' growth. The tangible tools that we recommend to use within your resources will be over a hundred, and they will be either temporary or permanent, because our industry changes almost on a weekly basis.

For now, **statcounter** will serve you very well, since it will give you a wealth of information about visitors to your website.... including the visitor counts in Real Time. That is important because you will be testing different squeeze, also known as landing, pages, and this tool will show you how effective each one of them are.

To illustrate, there are differences between resources and tools. Your website is an Anchor resource, and statcounter is a tool that you will use within it.

The concepts and ideas that you will learn from the intangible part of our training are actually more important than the tangible resources that you'll be given. This training comes in the form of Collaboration.

What exactly does that mean?

That will be fully explained as we get into the advanced boxes, and if you are truly committed to being successful in the internet marketing business, it will be very exciting for you. It's the catalyst that propels you from Zero to Success.

At this point, (assuming that you HAVE been working on the basics), it is time to monetize your business and have some cash flowing into a PayPal account. Let's start this within the next few days!

First, here's a little insight about what you're going to learn:

Two years ago Rich was looking into how to make a fairly reliable stream of income, in order to fund some of the tools that he would need to ramp up his Internet Marketing Business, He started by focusing on web hosting, autoresponders, web-site development, etc, etc. The things you have to spend money on.

However, if he were to spend his own hard earned money, he typically would tend to break out in a rash. So, for health reasons, he felt that it would be best to use other people's money (all of our partners need to embrace this concept), because it's never fun to hang out with a bunch of folks with rashes.

Well, after a lot of leg work a very simple way of doing this was discovered. We call it the "Craigslist—eBay Correlation." Once you start to use it, it will become income producing right away (usually within 3 days). It will be five bucks here, ten bucks there, however, it will all add up in a surprising way.

Once systematized, it can be handled by an admin. It can be completed by spending 30 minutes on the CL/eBay correlation every morning, while having the morning coffee. It can earn as much as $700.00 monthly as passive income.

This is called…STRM funding. Let's get started on this right away in Box 12. But before proceeding, do us a favor and send an email at richardmckelvey@msn.com, and let us know your most important business goal for the next full year, how long you have been in the internet business, and if you have had any success.

Time to get to work folks; we are burning daylight here.

Rich & Marty.

P.S..... STRM funding means......Straight to Rich & Marty.

BOX 12

E-A-R-N-I-N-G

Cha-Ching! How sweet the sound.

Well folks, since you are reading box 12, you came through the goal process, and we are glad to see you here.

OK, as we said at the close of Box 11, we want you to be effective and start earning right away. We now will blueprint the fastest method for you. The easiest (when you know how) way to create your earning stream on the internet is through affiliate marketing.

However, this is a very intricate part of your overall marketing plan. It is misunderstood by about 98% of those that participate in it. You must keep in mind that this is simply a small part of building your "Online Assets," but it can develop into a very lucrative part of it.

Start with this core theory: **"Find the NEED for a product, then put the product in front of the proper audience."** It does sound elementary, doesn't it? But you would be surprised how many marketers (98%) do it just the opposite way.

We mentioned the Craigslist—eBay connection. Let's start. Using Craigslist is a very simple process, even if you have never used it; try going there and playing around a bit (www.craigslist.com). It's a lot of fun and very entertaining.

If you feel overwhelmed by it, drop us an email, and we will walk you through it. This process is called the:

"Affiliate Re-Direct Method"

You can set up this method totally free of any charges by just doing email links, but we would highly recommend that you put up a generic type website with a cheap web-host. It will cost you about $10.00 dollars monthly, but you will make that many times over.

This is even more appealing when you train your admin the correct way, since it creates a "cash cow". The main reason for this is because Craigslist does not allow you to post Clickbank or eBay links within your ad responses; it is a violation of their terms of service. However, you CAN set up a simple redirect link from your website (which is allowed by Craigslist) to your affiliate site.

Step 1: There are two accounts that you will need to get started: a) a Clickbank account, and b) an eBay Affiliate Program Account.

Both are free programs. If you don't already have these accounts, sign up directly at www.clickbank.com and search for Affiliate by Conversion (formerly Commission Junction)to sign up for the eBay Affiliate Program.

OK, now that you have your accounts in place, go to Craigslist and go to the "For Sale" column. You will find it about ¾ of the way down the list, and you will see the "wanted" category. Just open this up and start reading what the people who posted here are looking for. (Does Find the NEED sound familiar here?).

Example: One day, my admin told me that there were a lot of people posting in "wanted" for a game called "Call to Duty, Black Ops". This is a game for the X-Box 360.

Well, at eBay our admin learned that the average price for this game, new in a box, was $69.00. Now this price is slightly lower than what most major retailers sell this game. It was generally priced in the $75.00 range. This was not enough of a discount to get anyone all excited.

So, by reaching into our little bag of tricks, and jumping over to one of our Gmail accounts, we went to Google Alerts (https://www.google.com/alerts), and typed in "Sale on Call to Duty Black Ops."

Note: This is a tool that has some far reaching effects for you, and you will be shown how in a later Box.

Within minutes' emails from "Google Alerts" were received (It is always a great pleasure for me to have the largest search engine in the world doing our work).

One of the alerts was from Toys R Us, and they put this game on sale for $49.95. This was the best price in all the alerts although many were close to this price. The game was in stock and ready for shipping. NOTE: It's a good practice to choose to stay with a nationally recognized store brand.

Afterwards, we went back to eBay, and typed "Toys R Us Coupons" in the search box.

Up popped 26 listings for discount coupons, and 20% off coupons were included. It was good on all regular and sale items, and it sold for $1.00. (Buy it now price).

Pause........How many of you knew that coupons are a huge business on eBay???? (There's more information about this in a later Box.)

Continue......So, then I went to Notepad and wrote up the offering (please note that when I say "I", it really means my admin did it).

Note: KISS Formula in play here. (cut and paste)

Hi, I was looking for the same item when I saw your ad. I don't have one to sell, but I found a great deal on this game at Toys R Us on eBay, and you can get a 20% discount coupon for it on eBay also, (insert coupon link) bringing the cost down to $40.96, including the dollar for the coupon. Here is the link for you (insert your affiliate hyperlink). I love this game, and I am always willing to help out a fellow gamer.

Regards, Richard.

Now, I had my admin open Craigslist, and go to the top 15 cities (remember folks, we are global), and cut and paste the Notepad reply to all the people looking for this item. She sent out close to one hundred Notepad replies, and my Clickbank report showed that this resulted in 7 sales, for a total commission of $32.41.

Now, you might say to yourself, $32.41 doesn't exactly shake the world up. But, stop and think for a moment.

This was one promotion, that took about 15 minutes to complete, and this was one item, upon hundreds to choose from. When you are running a couple of items every day, you will see that it does not take long to see some very significant dollars rolling into your Clickbank account.

This is the Craigslist side of the "Affiliate Redirect Method."

In Box 12B, we will go to the Clickbank side of the Method, and we will walk you through the direct promotion from Clickbank Affiliates to the Craigslist audience. This way, you will see how the triangle between Craigslist-eBay and Clickbank work to keep the dollars rolling in for you.

OK folks, you have some accounts to set up and some promotions to run. So let's stop getting ready to get ready; you now have work to do, and we are burning daylight here.

Rich and Marty.

PS. If there is any part of the process that you need help on, just drop us an email and we will help you out with it.

BOX12-B

E-A-R-N-I-N-G

C ha-Ching! ....An ancient oriental mantra to prevent body crashes :)

In the first part of Box 12 you learned how to search for the items that people were looking for.

Hence, find the need (niche) and fill the need.

Simple right? Or so you think now...that is because you are now in the tiny percentage of internet marketers that do it correctly.

By now, you should have set up a system and passed this task off to your admin. This will be the first of your many passive multiple income streams.

It has long been established that affiliate marketing is the easiest way to start monetizing your business. This is true, to an extent.

If it is the easiest way, then why do over 98% of the marketers who take this route still fail.

The answer is both simple and complex at the same time, a true conundrum.

They fail because they work through the system backwards, and, after a few months of seeing either poor or no results, they simply give up.

Don't fault them, or blame them for their actions. They do not understand that there are multiple phases of selling a product on-line.

As pointed out in Box 2, you are going to take your evolution from novice to pro. Remember, the subheading way back in Box 2 is **"Maximum Success is Achieved in Steps"**.

You have taken the first step in Box 12. Now that you are ready to engage in Affiliate Marketing,
you have the first of the income streams working for you already.

However, before we go to full Affiliate Marketing, we are going to go back to the other side of the Craigslist-eBay connection.

Affiliate Redirect Method: Part 2

For Part2, we are going to place free ads on Craigslist. In order to make this work, you'll need to create a fairly generic website URL, hosted on a cheap web hosting site.

This because Craigslist does not allow you to post an ad with an affiliate link in the ad. However, they do allow you to post your own domain name in the ad (go figure)!

Take Action! ...

Step 1: Set up a simple redirect connection from your website to your affiliate promotion in Clickbank (we have a full page tutorial on our website to help you set up a redirect connection). The Affiliate Site will take over and do all the work for you, and you get paid directly from Clickbank.

With the average affiliate commission of $30 to $50 per sale, it is a no brainer to see that the generic web site and the hosting are earned back on the very first sale.

Also, the reason you need a generic website URL, (example: www. infoyouneed.com) you will be sending buyers to many different affiliate sites, depending what you are promoting that week.

It only takes a minute to change your redirect from your generic site to a different affiliate program.

Currently Rich and I use 4 different generic website URLs and rotate them once a week, after checking our Clickbank commission page. If there's a lot of activity on one particular product, that ad will keep running as other generic URLs are added into the same affiliate program. The admins will run the ads indifferent cities in the same region.

This only takes a few minutes to complete and creates your second source income stream!

Now here comes the fun part. You don't have to rack your brains to find out what affiliate programs are hot at any particular moment in time.

Go to Clickbank and login into your account. Click on "Marketplace." Use the "Advance Search" option. On the dropdown menu you will see an option to search by "Gravity" (Gravity is a numerical representation of the activity and earnings of that product). You can filter to search by Gravity number. You want to look at products that have a Gravity number above 65.

Another option is to check our weekly emails. You'll find our list of the affiliate programs that are pulling in high numbers. Marty updates the list every 72 hours. We show you our top 5 choices on the list, and give you the reasons behind our play.

In the comment box at the bottom of the email you can see what your fellow marketers are saying about the affiliates they are promoting and what results they are seeing. We encourage everyone to participate in this open forum. It helps if everyone shares information, either positive or negative.

Check out the following statistics:

> 2011 E-Commerce Sales (excluding travel) were $ 194.3 billion dollars.
> 2012 E-Commerce Sales were $ 225.0 billion dollars.
> 2013 E-Commerce Sales were $ 252.0 billion dollars.
> 2014 E-Commerce Sales were $ 270.6 billion dollars.
> 2014 E-Commerce Sales (Worldwide) 2.356 Trillion Dollars.

Now these numbers were not just put here to wow you. They were shared to illustrate that the industry you have chosen is a solid, steady growth of revenue that will continue for many years into the future. As of first quarter 2015, the average annual growth rate is 16%.

As of August 2015, Amazon has passed Walmart as the largest retailer in the United States.

You have to decide for yourself, what percentage of this spending is going to belong to **you.**

How are you going to invest in yourself in order to ensure that you will be the profitable part of this equation?

What path will you take to secure for yourself the knowledge to be a true success in your chosen industry?

Many people will tell you that "knowledge is power", this is only partially true.

Applied Knowledge is power....

Because you can certainly be the smartest guy on the block, but if you do not correctly apply the knowledge you have, you will also be the smartest guy on the block, who is broke.

(Note: the word "broke" is, by far, the most profane word in the English language).

O.k. you've done your action steps, you now have a second income stream ready to roll, and this can be a very lucrative income stream.

However, the income stream doesn't stop here. There's a trick you will learn about adding AdSense income to your generic websites. And you will find out how to build a "Review" site, that is totally approved by Google, and earns you AdSense income, PPC income, and builds you a great niche mailing list as a bonus.

So, in Box 13 (lucky), we will generate income streams 4, 5 and 6. You will see that it is always fun adding income streams. But for now, folks, you have work to do; so let's stop getting ready to get ready. We are burning daylight here.

See you all on the other side of Box 13.

Rich and Marty

BOX 13

"CRAPAPEDIA"

A t the end of Box12-B we said that we would go on to income streams 4, 5 and 6. By all means we will, and we will add many more income streams beyond that. First, let's walk through a tutorial to bring us back into focus.

The original intentions for income streams 1, 2, and 3 are now obvious. They exist solely to bring you to the realization that income can be generated through the internet. By now, you should be seeing some of your efforts being turned into cash flow.

These streams also exist because it is a lot easier to re-invest in your business if you are using generated dollars, rather than dollars from your own pocket.

You may also be getting the point that these income streams are basically one-time customer deals. Meaning that, once a person buys from you through one of your affiliate programs, there is no way of knowing if you will ever see this customer again.

Not to say that is a bad thing, you can roll up a nice income just doing these type of deals.

However, this is why the phrase **"Crapapedia"** was coined. (This phrase was sort of stolen from Wikipedia).

How many times have you heard that you must build an email list, to create a sustainable long term business?

This is very true, but not the whole picture. To truly succeed, you need to create a **focused list** in your target market.

Undoubtedly, you have seen quite a few pitches throughout the internet for the next "greatest fully automated software developed" to skyrocket your email list into the tens of thousands.

These pitches usually include a screenshot of their Clickbank account that shows they are raking in thousands with this method. (Crapapedia!)

The irony here is that they are making that money from you, because you are their target list. These guys are mega-marketers who share their lists with EACH OTHER. Then they EACH bombard you with emails and you "better act because they are taking it off the market in XXXX number of hours/days." (Crapapedia!)

These so-called marketers are masters of the "law of large numbers", and everything they sell only belongs in one file, yes, the Crapapedia file.

.

So, how do we separate ourselves from these groveling Crapapedia peddlers????

We create our own focused list, within a niche that we have an actual *passion* for, and that we are willing to work with over the long term to maximize revenue. This will be a list that we are going to deliver genuine value to, so that everyone we come into contact with *benefits* from our efforts.

This is what is known in the internet as establishing **"Authority."**

And when you are established as an "authority" (expert), you'll gain the most valuable form of currency on the planet, **"Influence."**

The big daunting question is: How do I become this "Authority" and gain "Influence?!"

You Focus.

> You pick a market you want to establish yourself as a leading expert. Re: Health and Wellness, Vintage Clothing, Fitness Training, Martial Arts, Dating, Holistic Healing, Green Products, Parrot Training, etc., etc. and all the sub-categories that come into each and every target market.

> You develop a top notch commanding Squeeze Page (a one-page website or landing page, see below) that gathers the emails of people who are interested in the products and services within that market.

> You create an authority website that is content rich, provides value, gives credible advice, and solves people's problems.

> And you NEVER, we repeat, NEVER sell anything on your Authority site.

That's right folks, now that you know what you have to do, it's time to get all our ducks in a row.

Now, for those of you who might not be familiar with or know exactly what a Squeeze Page is...

No matter what you have learned in the past, or what some Crapapedia peddler has tried to sell you, **a Squeeze page is simply a one-page website**. Period.

And it only has **one purpose**. It is created to gather the name and email address of your potential clients. Never try, or even hint, that you are selling something on your squeeze page, if you do, you will defeat its entire purpose.

In order to induce someone to give you their name and email address, you must give them something in value in return. It can be in the form of a report, a free E-book, a product (promo), or any item or information product that YOUR target market wants or needs.

The value you give them, must be genuine and original, and it MUST be engaging. It must be powerful enough for your list to want to hear from you again.

Remember, the email address is the **"currency of the world wide web,"** and people will give you their currency if they perceive they are getting value in exchange for it.

Take Action...

Step 1: Go to www.yola.com, sign up for a free account, and start building your Squeeze Page. Take your time, play with it, tweak it, and have fun with it. Your original squeeze page will take on its own evolution.

Step 2: When you have finished your Squeeze Page Project, send us a link. We will take a look at it, and send you our thoughts and recommendations. We will also put it on our 20 Group forum, and ask all the participants to give an opinion. If, at some point, you decide that you want to be part of our group, you'll be asked to do this for someone else.

Later on, we will show you all the tips and tricks to make you Squeeze Page a powerful conversion machine geared to your own target audience. You will learn how to use our Landing Page Optimization that is quite unique in its approach and performance. The results will be measurable through your autoresponder. This is exciting and eye opening stuff.

So now folks, you have work to do. Stop getting ready to get ready; we are burning daylight here,

Rich and Marty

BOX 14

SOLOPRENEURS AND CHICKENPRENEURS

The great majority of folks, who enter and then act in Internet Marketing, attempt to do it as one of these two types...

Let me explain why most Solopreneurs (you) turn into Chickenpreneurs...

When a person enters this field on their own, they do not realize the vast amount of knowledge that is necessary to compete. Nor, do they realize the tremendous amount of time that is necessary to gather all of the information and resources needed to be successful.

Let's give you an example:

Imagine that your website is all built and ready to go. You need traffic to your site, so you have decided to begin with Article writing. You want to see if people will notice and click on your link and visit your site.

You might take the following steps and go to:

1. EzineArticles -The big daddy of article directories. If you could only choose one place to submit your articles, this would be a good choice. PR6 (PR is short for <u>Page Ranking</u>. It is a grading system, that ranks websites between 1 and 10. It was devised and adopted by Google to rank the sites on the internet using a formula of their own.)
2. GoArticles -This one claims to be the largest, but #1, #3, and #4 gives it a run for its money. PR4
3. WebProNews -You have to be selected to get into this one, but it's well worth the trouble. It's old and respected. PR6
4. Contribute to a blog. (Preferred for article writing). A lot of blogs out there accept guest posts. What knowledge do you have to share related to your niche business? Publish it and send it to blogs or websites that are looking for content. **Make sure that you ask them to include your bio and hyperlink it to your site.**

What can be sharing your knowledge get you? If you gain at least one new customer from an article (but hopefully you'll get lots more) it's worth it. And it will help your credentials and boost your authority.

WOW, you say to yourself.

Which one of the above do I choose? Which one will give me the best exposure, which one is free, and which ones cost me money? How can I check all these out and make sure I am using the right one?

Hey folks…welcome to the next level of information overload.

Now, to continue our example, you have likely realized that this project needs more research before you come back to it. So you decide to switch to optimizing your website in order drive more targeted traffic that you need.

However, you're not sure where to start this process, EITHER. Maybe you try seeking out SEO directories, then find out, heck, you don't have to do that. Apparently, only a few are still around after the Panda (a recent update of their algorithm) update.

However, before you even glance at them, here's a word of warning:

The algorithm changes in Google during 2014 heavily leaned toward penalizing sites that use directories. The 5 exceptions are:

Google
DMoz
Yahoo
Bing
YouTube

(For now, stick with the top 5 above. You know them as search engines, but they fully function as directories also. We will fully explain and show you how to use the above search engines as directories in a future Box, and you will begin to understand how this all comes together.)

Wow, you say: Where do I start, how do I use these directories, which ones will give me the best results............ AHHHHHHHHHHHHHHH...............

Are you getting the point yet? Or is this being too subtle?!

This may be one of the points in the process where a Solopreneur becomes a Chickenpreneurs.

This is where information overload kicks in and where 96% of the start-ups just simply give up and leave. This is the point where the person without a guide starts the slide to failure.

Luckily, there is a Solution.

We Call It the "DDP Factor"

1)Desire. 2) Dedication. 3) Perseverance.

Having expounded on these qualities in previous boxes, you can appreciate that these are the qualities that are absolutely necessary for success. Our internet marketing business demands it.

You have just browsed through many places today, and been given a lot of food for thought. Box 15 is a blueprint for "Taking Action Towards your Goals", with a bunch of really cool resources.

Meanwhile, if you have any pressing problem that you are faced with, you can always drop an email at richard@ internetvisionsdefined.com or marty@ internetvisionsdefined.com, and we will be more than happy to send you some solutions.

Folks, we have work to do here, so stop getting ready to get ready. We are burning daylight here!

See you all in Box 15.

Rich and Marty

BOX 15

FIELD OF DREAMS
(NOT EXACTLY)

"BUILD IT AND THEY WILL COME"
(NOT EXACTLY)

BUILD IT AND *SHOW* THEM HOW TO COME
(EXACTLY)

A s stated in previous boxes, 99% of "wanna be" and "experienced" Internet Marketers approach their marketing efforts backwards. They build a web site based on **their** idea of the product they want to promote, and then they have to figure out whom to sell it to and how to sell it to them.

Good ideas aren't as common as stupid people think they are.

What they haven't figured out is the simplest of all formulas. There are literally millions of people out in cyberspace searching for something.

Why then, do you not go to them and discover and learn what they are searching for?

The formula is simple:

Do KEYWORD research
Create your SEO around those Keywords
Develop focused content
Build your site

You have now reversed the "Field of Dreams" theory. Let your target market "tell" you what to build, and then go ahead and build it for them. Then they WILL come! You just have to show them the road to get there (SEO).

So, let us start with Keyword research:

The first and most important thing to remember is that without the **PROPER** keywords and keyword phrases you have nothing: no traffic, no visits, no views, no page rank, no nada, no nothing. Let's rephrase that so you understand. You have **NOTHING.**

We cannot over emphasize how important keyword research is. It is the lifeblood of all your efforts. If you don't make the effort to create a support structure for your keyword research and you are not willing to put in the time and effort, then don't bother at all. Because "no keyword research" means "no SEO"; it can't be done without it. Keywords are the absolute building blocks of SEO.

So to get a #1 placement in search engines, the first and the most important step is to choose the right keywords and key-phrases for which you want to rank first.

The box below contains an excerpt from the book "Acres of Diamonds" by Russell Conwell and it was written in 1921. Even though this was written 90 years ago, it certainly sounds like it was written this year to explain Internet Marketing.

> The seeds of fortune are close at hand. Stick with what you know, find your niche, and don't be swayed by the allure of "greener pastures."
>
> Find out what people want, and fill that need. This sounds obvious, but many entrepreneurs start with a product or service, and then try to find a market for their product or service. Conwell advises finding the market first, then developing a product or service to meet that demand.
>
> Make the best possible product and provide them to a large number of people. You have now done your research and found there are a significant amount of monthly searches for a particular product. It could be anything, this doesn't matter.

So, let us begin with your keyword selection.

Take Action…

Step 1: Write down what you believe online searchers would type into their browser for your selected product.

Step 2: Ask people you know what would they type into a search engine to find a particular product that you have an interest in creating a niche for. Make sure to include ALL the keywords people suggest to you in your research list. Even though some of them may sound a little strange to you. You need to understand that keywords are multi-generational, multi-cultural and multi-regional.

EXAMPLE: A25-year-old fellow wanted to buy a fairly good set of stereo headphones, (Bose quality) so he typed **"Quality Headphones"** into his browser.

Then his Mom thought it was a good idea to buy her son this as a birthday gift, so she typed **"Quality Headsets"** into her browser.

His Dad had the same idea, and since he is 10 years older than her, he naturally typed **"Quality Hi-Fi Earphones"** into his browser.

Then his 21-year-old brother wanted to see if he could buy a set for himself, so he typed **"Quality Wireless Headphones"** into his browser.

So, you see, 4 different people from the same family, looking for the same exact product, entered 4 different keywords based on their own personal experience. Now a quick Google search for the keyword "Headphones" produced a global monthly search of 3,350,000. This was by far the leading keyword.

However, Headsets received 368,000 searches, Earphones received 450,000 searches and Wireless Headsets and Earphones produced 500,000 searches. Conclusion: If you exclude the 2nd. 3rd& 4th keywords, you also exclude 1,318,000 searches for the same basic product.

Step 3: Create a spreadsheet to track and analyze the competition in your niche. Go to Google and do a search for the Keywords and/or Key-phrases that you wish to rank for. Select only the top 5 ranking sites on the Google results and note the address for these sites in your spreadsheet.

Step 4: Open each site individually. On the site's main page, right click your mouse, and on the drop down menu that appears, scroll down to "view source". Click on that and a website analysis page will appear.

Step 5: In the box on the far right, "Description" write the number of times that their Keywords and Key phrases appear in the very first paragraph of their homepage.
(this is important).

For example, assume that the #1 ranked site has a keyword listed 4 times, and the #2 & 3 ranked sites have it 5 times, and the #4 & 5 ranked sites have it 6 times. Well, it's obvious where Google is going with this. This gives us a view on Google's sensitivity to Keyword stuffing in their algorithm.

Now, once we have all this information, we want to compare it to the Keywords and Key-phrases that we have selected.

Image # 4 Box 15

URL	Keyword	MetaTa	H1	H2	Descriptio
www.etc					
www.abc					
www.def					
www.ghi					
www.jkl					

The top 6 ranked sites have obviously done their Keyword research, otherwise they would not be on the first page of Google. (In a resource lesson later on you will see how to find out the history of how long a particular website has been ranked on the Google first page).

This is important information to know in order to judge the **sustainability of your Keywords.**

Once all your keyword data is collected, select the top 10 strongest Keywords used by these sites. These 10 will become the basis of what you insert in your page source, after combining your Keywords and doing further analytics on more advanced sites than Google. Once that is completed, we will be able to determine the 7 strongest Keywords available to you. We have all the advanced sites listed in the member's area of our website, and this is free access to all 20 Group members.

Our 20 Groups are formed for non-competing business persons to grow their businesses by meeting with like-minded members. It is a collaborative learning and networking process that stimulates working together with the other members to see what has been successful and works best for others. With this platform you are in business for yourself, but not by yourself.

If you need assistance your group admin will be happy to walk you through any questions on the phone.

Just to make it clear, we are only talking about and participating in ORGANIC SEARCH, which is the most powerful of all traffic (client) driving systems. You can very quickly go broke, if you research the most powerful Keywords, and then use them in paid advertising such as a PPC or Google Ad-Word campaign.

Google is well aware of the power of these Keywords, and charges a premium to use them in paid campaigns. You could easily burn through 3 to 4 thousand dollars in a PPC campaign, to return sales of 2 thousand dollars. Damn, we feel a rash coming on!

In Box 16, we go through the next 5 steps to complete your web site SEO. This is "Gotta have it stuff."

So folks, stop getting ready to get ready; we are burning daylight here. We will see you all on the other side in Box 16.

Rich and Marty

BOX 16

HOLISTIC SEO

As we continue onto the next steps in search engine optimization, we use the word **Holistic** in its purest form. On the other hand, we are completely opposed to any "black hat" tactics of gaining pagerank by using linking services. In the long run that they will do more damage to your SEO efforts than they will do good. "Black Hat" SEO refers to using techniques or tricks, such as keyword stuffing, that, at best, use short term strategies to get better search engine recognition. **You run the risk of being penalized by search engines.** Just don't use them!

They gather weak and irrelevant sites to link to you, and this would be recognized by Google and cause you grief in the end.

So keep it clean, put in the extra hard work, and it will give you the results that you desire.

In the resource box, at our "20 Group" site, there is a concise and complete blueprint that outlines step by step the best SEO procedures. Since this is a real time consuming effort, you can designate your admin to this task and free up your time.

All readers of "Internet Marketing Defined" are granted free access to the 20 Group resources.

Battleground Changes

Just about 1 years ago, Google made sweeping changes to its algorithms, and a lot of people were caught off guard. Take a look at the list below and see how the page ranking of some of the most influential websites across all industries were affected:

- Search Engine Roundtable (from 7 to 4)
- Blog Herald (from 6 to 4)
- Weblog Tools Collection (from 6 to 4)
- JohnTP (from 6 to 4)
- Coolest Gadgets (from 5 to 3)
- CyberNet News (from 6 to 4)

It looks like mainstream websites that were selling links were also penalized:

- Washington Post (from 7 to 5)
- Washington Times (from 6 to 4)
- Charlotte Observer (from 6 to 4)
- Forbes.com (from 7 to 5)
- SFGate.com (from 7 to 5)
- Sun Times (from 7 to 5)
- New Scientist (from 7 to 5)
- Seattle Times (from 6 to 4)

Google ranks pages on a scale of 1-10, with 10 being the strongest. You can see just how much the changes in their algorithms hurt these sites.

Hundreds and hundreds of hours of hard work by these businesses web teams vanished with the "click of a mouse." If the above powerhouses were badly affected, just think of your site and how poorly it would stand up against these giants.

A small change in the algorithms may well put your site about 35 miles west of Siberia.

Google has also announced that these changes will be an ongoing process to improve user experience and eliminate black hat tricks from ranking pages higher. Google is out to protect their virtual real estate, and they will always win against underhanded black hat tactics.

With that out of the way, let us get started on the *real* process of SEO.

In box 15 we explained how to build your website to make its foundations SEO efficient.

Now we would like to explain the process to start you on the way to Google's top page ranking.

You must have only ONE target goal: **To land on the first page of Google.**

All efforts must be driven with this result in mind. Without being on the first page of Google, think of yourself as a portable heater salesman, and your territory is the Sahara Desert (you get the picture).

OK, now that your website foundation is built and ready to go, you need to get your site indexed.

Please understand that, if you had your website built by a third party, it is most likely that they did not do this. Nor did they enter any keywords that will be effective in the source code, unless you gave them specific instructions, and paid the SEO fees to have keywords entered.

Take Action…

Step 1: Index your site by listing it in our top 5 web directories (and the # 1 directory is DMOZ.) The drawback to listing on DMOZ is that it takes a lot of time for your site to be reviewed and included.

You can get a listing of all possible website directories in the addendum we have relating to Box 14. However, at this point, as of the April 21, 2015 Google update, we are advising against directory listings beyond the top 5 previously noted.

Members of one of our 20 Groups are running tests to see the effectiveness of using other directory listings as of this date. You can follow the test results at the site in the SEO resource area of our website.

Step 2: Get your site registered with a pinging service. We use pingler.com. They charge about $2.00 per month for automatic pinging about every 2-3days.

The purpose of a pinging service is to send out notifications to Google spiders to crawl your website to see new information and site upgrades. We'll explain in a future box exactly what the spiders are looking for and how to configure your site to be "SEO spider-friendly."

Now let's "beef up" your site.

One of the little know Google "quirks" is that they place very little importance on what they term "thin" websites. So, if you have published the basic 4 or 5-page website, now is the time to start adding pages. No one knows the exact number of pages that Google designates as "not thin"; some SEO experts say 20 or more, and some SEO experts say the number is 50. We believe that between 25 and 50 pages or more is correct.

For instance, after a search for the generic term "dog training", the #1 ranked website had 19 pages and the # 2 website had 41 pages.

Step 3: (Very Important) Go to the top websites in your niche market (using your keywords) and get an average number of total pages for the sites that you will be competing against.

If you are a Twenty Group member, login, go to the information box, and use our step by step formula for adding pages to your website. You will also find out how to rank the pages in order of importance.

Let's recap here for a moment:

- We have done our keyword research
- Built our site foundation based on the keywords
- Added our content
- Completed our SEO on the website

Then:

- You indexed our site with the directories
- Registered our site with a pinging service
- Started to add pages to our site

So we bet you believe that you're almost done, huh?

SORRY, YOU ARE NOT EVEN CLOSE TO DONE.
(but you ARE actually way ahead of 98% of your competition)

The good news though is that you're off to a great start.

Before signing off today's box, here is one very important thought. *Don't even think* of trying to rank your website based on *single* key words.

You will never get to the first page of Google trying to rank for single words; maybe you'll get to page 10 or 12...if you're lucky.

In **Box 17**, as you go a little deeper into SEO, we will show you how to use keyword combinations to move up in the page rankings. You will also find out where to research these keyword combinations for your market niche.

Also, we will be diving into your back linking campaign to find out how and why it is of the "utmost" importance to your page rank advancement tactics.

With that thought, it is time to stop getting ready to get ready. We are burning daylight here folks; get to work and we'll see you on the other side in BOX 17.

BOX 17

HOLISTIC SEO II

Of course it is perfectly clear:

H ere is a point that you must clearly understand: Google, MSN, Yahoo or any other search engine will **NEVER** go out and look for your website.

That is not what they do. They have never done that. And they won't start now.

The ONLY purpose of a search engine is to database information. When someone types in a query (asks a question) for the search engine, it goes into its database and retrieves the information that it has indexed and shows it to you. It is a simple as that. There's no need to get more complicated.

Now you ask, how *does* the information gets into the search engine database?

Answer: **YOU** put it there. **YOU** have to show the search engine spiders how to get to **YOUR** information. It is as simple as that.

Although the purpose, the question, and the answers are all simple, the process itself is complicated.

That is what makes it challenging. We'll teach you how to take the process and make it systemic.

Previously we have explained the basics of SEO. Now we will explain the advanced parts. The SINGLE most important part of your search engine optimization are LINKS.

Internal links, external links, backlinks, outbound links, inbound links, no matter what type they are, they are all links. **Links are all important**.

First, visualize links as a set of railroad tracks:

Then visualize the Google spiders as the locomotive:

And the links YOU choose are going to send that Locomotive Spider along those railroad tracks at high speed, with no detours, directly into the heart of your railroad station.(your website).

Now this is the most important part of your linking strategy.

You see, the locomotive will travel to you as long as the direction remains TRUE.

It followed the track from a site that is relevant to your industry niche, to your subject matter, and to your content. It followed a TRUE path. It stayed on the track.

When the locomotive arrives at your station site, and sees that the content you have (keywords, meta-tags, headers, body copy,) is complementary to the station site it just came from, (similar keywords, phrases, etc.) it automatically knows it is on the right track, gathers all the information (passengers) from your site, brings it back to the main terminal (database), and offloads (indexes) it all there.

However, if the locomotive leaves a health food station or a martial arts station or a parrot training station and pulls into your station, and finds no content that fits the images it just left, the locomotive backs out of your station and takes no passengers (information) with it.

Hence, worthless railroad links (broken tracks). If the locomotive makes too many of these trips, it eventually closes your station for repairs.

The analogy that was presented may seem a little contrite to some of you, but it illustrates exactly how the process of indexing your website content is performed by search engines.

Once you understand how they work, and what their job is, it makes it a lot clearer for you to understand the relevance and importance of your linking campaign.

So, let us expand your linking campaign...

OK, by now you should have completed making directory listings, which you will continue to do at the rate of about 2-3 per week.

Now, start a new spreadsheet and you can call it "Competition Backlinks."

Take Action...

Step 1: Go to Google and type in the keywords and/or the key-phrases that you are looking to rank for.

Example: If you would type in Training Parrots, it would give you the first page of Google rankings for the key-phrase Training Parrots.

Step 2: Copy the URL's of the top 5 sites, and paste them into your spreadsheet.

Step 3: DO NOT stop here. Continue by repeating using variations on your keywords and key phrases.

Example: Training Parrots to talk, Teaching Parrots to talk, Talking Parrots, Training Parrots to Speak, Speaking to Parrots, etc.

Step 4: With keyword variations, many of the sites that you saw on the first attempt will appear again. Look for the ones that are new to the list for different keywords and key-phrases.

At this point, you should have a list on your spreadsheet for at least the top 10 websites that are in competition for your keywords and key-phrases.

Step 5: Go to the Yahoo browser, (this only works on Yahoo) and in the search bar type in Link:http://_____.com (insert the websites from your spreadsheet in the blank).

This will bring up all the sites that are linking to your competitors. On the right side of the list you will see a box that says "Explore". Click on that box and it will give you all the details of the link. Copy all these links and into your spreadsheet.

Step 6: Ignore any backlink that comes from an article or from an article directory, these will be very weak 3rd-Party backlinks, and not worth the effort to link into them.

Make sure to look for genuine relevant websites that your competition has links to. Always keep in mind that these sites have landed on the first page of Google because they did their homework on SEO and have the qualified backlinks that can a valuable resource for you.

Step 7: Many of these sites will be blogs and social media bookmarking sites. Log into any and all that you can and leave relevant comments or post meaningful content. In return, you receive the same back-links that your competition has. Since you will be researching many different websites, you will be able to build a much stronger back linking base aggregated from all the top sites.

Step 8: Put your back linking efforts on your schedule for 1 hour per day for the first 2-3 weeks. You need to make all back-linking appear to be a natural organic flow, rather than clumped into a one or two-day period.

If you are a guest member of our 20 Group site, we have a tool for you in the resource area that automates all the above processes and can run on autopilot. This will save you countless hours in your back linking campaign.

At this juncture, you have enough tasks to keep you busy for several days, as you are setting up your spreadsheets and farming backlinks.

When we go into **Box 18**, we will be teaching you some very advanced SEO techniques known as "Footprint Chronicles" and "Latent Semantic Indexing" (LSI). Plus, we will delve into the Social Bookmarking arena, which will become a very important part of your SEO campaign.

At times some of you are bound to get a little intimidated with all the information and processes that are strange and new to you. It is not our intent to either confuse or overwhelm you with information.

We promise that all the pieces will fall into place shortly, and will become a matter of routine.

Many of the steps that we teach have fully automated programs that you can apply to make all these tasks very simple. Our 20Group site provides all these resources for you, and we invite you to come and examine all the free resources that will benefit you.

So folks, we have to stop getting ready to get ready, and you have a lot of work to do. We are burning daylight here, so we will see you on the other side of **Box 18.**

BOX 18

HOLISTIC SEO PART III

"...THE OBJECTIVE IS NOT TO "MAKE YOUR LINKS APPEAR NATURAL"; THE OBJECTIVE IS THAT YOUR LINKS ARE NATURAL."

- Matt Cutts

Go gle

At this point you should have a fairly good idea of what is involved in the entire SEO process.

It's understandable that when you started to learn the basics of SEO you would not have believed how involved it really is. There is an abyss of information that surrounds it and at times it seems overwhelming.

Not to worry! It will all tie together as we keep putting the pieces together. Just know that a comprehensive link-building campaign to get your website to rank on Google's first page will take about six months, if it is done in a natural manner.

During this six-month period, you will have to put in a lot of work. You must, at all costs, **avoid going to a paid link-building service**. They will produce so many zero-page rank links that more harm than good will come from this type of activity.

Do the work, put in the time, and you will reap the justifiable rewards. It is as simple as that.

At this point you must be thinking that everyone talks about getting backlinks but no one explains on exactly how to get them. Well let us explain it to you!

The first step in backlink farming is to build your own brand first. (Brand link). This is an essential tactic that is so extremely overlooked that it never ceases to amaze us.

(A brand link is a link containing your brand name in the link's anchor text – this might include a link that just uses your URL as the link text.) Instead of linking as <u>bad credit loans</u>, you probably want to link YourCompanyName.com or <u>Your Company Name</u> or <u>Your Site Name</u>

The truth is that marketers who skip link building are destined to spin their wheels in cyberspace, while those who embrace the process will propel their websites into a new realm of profitability.

On the internet, perception is more important than reality.

This is the only part of SEO that is about YOU.

In order to obtain quality backlinks that are relevant to your website and your business, your site visitors must know who you are. This needs to be evident in your URL and your Keywords; this needs to be your BRAND.

This is the one item (brand) you want to get known on all the social and business media sites.

You as a person, do not matter.... **You as a Branded** entity matters a lot.

EXAMPLE:

Would you like to get a back-link from Coca-Cola or from a guy named Muhtar Kent?

You see, Muhtar Kent, Chairman & CEO of Coca-Cola International, is one of the top business leaders in the world, and he really doesn't matter.

We're not trying to compare apples to oranges here. We do not expect you, as a small business person, to build a brand to the magnitude of a corporate giant.

However, you can build your brand into a **giant in your niche.**

You can develop yourself and your brand into the "go to" guy/gal in your industry segment. Then people and other brands will want to link to you, because you will have become the trusted source in your target market. **Google puts very high rankings on "trusted sources".**

This is how the sites that made it to the first page of Google for your target market got there.

They became trusted sources by people linking (which you will learn is a vote of confidence) to them.

The recent changes in the Google algorithms, known commonly as beginning with the Panda Effect, have shifted the emphasis away from the content marketers and onto the social media side of cyber-space. So, we will be directing about 40% of our back linking efforts in these areas.

Let us start by putting a different twist on article marketing. We instructed you in a previous box how to write an article and submit it to Articles.com or GoArticles.com and a host of other article aggregation sites.

It seems now that Google is placing a lot less authority on article sites.

So, in a move toward social media syndication, we want to put this information content out in cyberspace ourselves. You will find it more rewarding feeling proactive in your own SEO efforts, rather than waiting around to be picked up by an article generator. From now on, we'll be publishing differently.

Take Action…

Step 1: Write a blog or article in a basic text format. Save it with your keyword header. This will allow you to go back to it and change your keyword heading and body content to reuse the article in several different areas.

Make sure the title of your blog article entices your target audience to click on it, giving you a backlink from your blog article to your website, and the backlink now comes from a social media site.

Inside of your article create several hyperlinks to other pages on your website. Each time someone clicks on the hyperlinks it creates an internal backlink which helps in giving your site authority in the eyes of Google. (The natural way).

Your article must be void of self-promotion, and only give good solid advice in the content.

However, in keeping with the intent of writing the article in the first place, which is to gain visitors for your website, you MUST add signage buttons at the end of the article. The first one should be your brand URL, then add TweetThis, Facebook Like, LinkedIn Share and AddThis buttons. If you need assistance speak with your webmaster or drop us a note at Richard@internetvisionsdefined.com or Marty@ internetvisionsdefined.com

Step 2: Post the blog or article onto your website.

Step 3: Open a HubSpot account and put your blog or article up for publication. (HubSpot is an inbound marketing software platform that helps companies attract visitors, convert leads, and close customers.) Now, directly from HubSpot you can send out the notifications to Facebook and Twitter.

Step 4: Wait a day or two and then go to your Digg account and post the blog article there. Inform some of your friends and colleagues so they can go to Digg and Digg your article. Keep a track on the number of "Diggs" you receive for that blog article, and this will tell you if your keyword heading is compelling or not. You can always go to the edit function and improve the heading.

Step 5: Now, here is a tactic that is only used by advanced marketers: In addition to your social media syndication, you can do your own blog article submissions. There are thousands of Newsletters on the world wide web, in all different niches and markets, for health and beauty, for pet care, for horse training, for teaching parrots to talk, for raising children, for elder care, for religious beliefs, for non-religious beliefs, for sumo wrestling, for martial arts, or for any type of collectors you can think of. Well anyway, you get the big picture.

These Newsletters constantly need new and useful articles for their publications. Especially if they are a weekly or bi-monthly publication. They welcome your articles IF they are relevant to their niche Newsletter. Tag, or create a link to your blog article and let their subscribers get back to you. (**always Tag with the lead in of: If you want more information on this subject go to www.yourwebsite.com**)

Search Google newsletters that pertain to your particular target audience. Create a spreadsheet and database for particular Newsletters based on their number of subscribers, and the frequency at which they are published. Seek out Newsletters that are published at a minimum of twice a month, and are from a trusted source.

Example: If you are in the Pet Care Products niche, go tohttp://www.aspca.org/pet-care and go to their blog. You can write a review of one of their articles and then **add your website anchor text** to the comment box. This gives you a backlink from a powerful .org brand.

Step 6: Do this process a couple of times, and then write up an in-depth article that provides value. (For instance in the above example, an on how the recent Mississippi River floods have impacted animals both domestic and wild.) Submit the article through the "contact us" button on a Newsletter's page. Request that you be included in their "Ask the Experts" column as a regular contributor. This effort will pay big dividends in your niche target market.

Step 7: Once they publish your article, and let the world know about it, repeat the above process by letting your social media syndicate follow a path to your door.

You have just gained Authority by having your blog article published in a nationally known newsletter. Of course, you want to place a hyperlink on your website that leads back to the article on the ASPCA site. This is known as an outbound link, and it goes to a high ranking trusted source.

Google places value on outbound links to these sites in addition to the inbound link.

Creating quality niche content for other websites is smart marketing.

OK, folks, you have absorbed a little bit of information on back linking today. There is a whole bunch more to come, but, alas, we are burning daylight here; it is now time to stop getting ready to get ready, and do a little bit of homework.

We hope you enjoyed today's tidbits, and we look forward to seeing you on the other side of Box 19.

Here is to your success.

Rich and Marty.

BOX 19

CREATE***MARKET***MONETIZE

Now that we have gone through the SEO lessons in the last 3 boxes, let us show you the type and volume of work you will need to produce using your newly learned SEO skills.

There are 4 factors that need (mandatory) to be used in conjunction with your SEO efforts.

If you are unwilling or unprepared to take on the work that is necessary to complete your quest for # 1 Google page ranking, then now would be a good time to revisit our earlier boxes on affiliate marketing and continue going that route until you feel prepared to move forward.

The factors and statistics we are presenting for you now show a clear blueprint of what you must do to gain the visibility you need to be successful. These statistics are facts taken from surveys of over 5,000 business enterprises who use internet marketing to grow their business.

Let us be clear, so there is no confusion here.

1). You have researched and selected your keywords and key phrases that you wish to rank for.

2). You have built and fully optimized your site for these keywords.

3). All your social media sites are set and ready.

4). Your site is published or fully ready to be published.

In other words, you are set to go. Here are our mandatory 4 Factors:

Factor # 1——— Your Landing Page(s)

You'll need to create multiple landing pages for your website.

Surveys show that a business with 31 to 40 landing pages gets 7 times more views and leads than does a business with 1 to 5 landing pages.

A business with over 40 landing pages gets 12 times the views and leads than a business with 1 to 5 landing pages.

Do the math, this shows that the difference is so huge, that a lot of time and effort needs to go into building your landing pages.

Box 22, in our advanced series, will teach you how to build a compelling and converting landing page in under 15 minutes.

Factor # 2——— Your Blogging

You must Blog a minimum of 20 times a month. (for the first 3 months). A business that blogs 16 times a month gets twice the amount of traffic and leads than a business who blogs 4 or less times a month.

However, a business that blogs 20 times a month receives 5 times more traffic than a business that blogs 4 or less times a month.

This does not need to be a monumental task. You can set up your blog on your website, and daily blog posts should only take a few minutes, and can be delegated to your admin.

Your blog postings on your site will have the button apps for "Tweet" this and "Share" this on Facebook and "Share" this on LinkedIn. It will also have your RSS feed line, giving you a lot of exposure.

Businesses that had over 200 blog posts in their inventory (website) received 5.6 times more traffic and leads than a site that had 20 or less blog posts.

It is all about putting your brand out in front of your target audience. (Notice: it's your "brand" NOT "yourself" that's out in front).

So, get your blog up and running and always give valuable content.

Factor # 3—— Your Website.

Do not expect to launch a basic 5-page website and expect any great thing to happen. Nothing will happen. You have to make it happen. The minimum requirement for the Google spiders to take any real notice to your site is 25 to 50 pages.

The spiders love content, and they also love optimized content. Give them a reason to stay on your site, and they will happily oblige you.

Adding pages after you publish to the internet is called "building out your site", and if you are subscribed to a pinging service, as we will explain in more detail in Box 23, this will work to your advantage as you build out your site.

You should set your goal for building out your site to a minimum of 400 pages. Businesses with 400 or more website pages receive 9 times more traffic than websites that have between 50 to 100 pages.

As sure as night follows the day, the more visitors that your website produces, the more leads and conversions that will be produced for your business.

In Box 23 we take you step by step through the process of building out your site, teach you how and where to add pages to your site, and explain how to **optimize each page and their headings.** This will make the pages more attractive and friendly to the Google spiders.

Factor # 4—— Your Social Influence.

In the short time since Google has changed its algorithms to reflect a significant emphasis on social media, the results have shown to have had major impacts on sites across cyberspace.

More importantly, it has greatly leveled the playing field in which a dedicated internet marketer can go head to head with larger companies, and succeed in positioning yourself onto Google's page 1 search.

It is no longer a question of *should* we be involved in social media...it is a question of how do we become fully involved and create a massive social media reach.

The exponential effect of social media is unprecedented in its effect, more than any other form of advertising has ever accomplished before.

A business with 500 to 1,000 Facebook fans and Twitter followers received 3.5 more times more website traffic than did a business with 25 fans and followers.

However, a business with over 1,000 fans and followers received a staggering 22 times more website visits than did a business with 25 followers.

The social media reach in today's world simply cannot be overlooked or ignored. It is the driving force in internet marketing.

Take Action...

Step 1: Register at www.klout.com and index your social media stats at the beginning of your campaign. Then you will be able to benchmark your progress as you go along. Your goal here is to become an "Influencer" in all venues of social media in your market niche.

While social media is a numbers game, it must also be a "focused" numbers game. **It's more effective to have 300 focused fans or followers than 2,000 fragmented fans or followers.**

This is why we have designed Box 24 solely focused on the correct strategies to maximize your impact on the social media world. It is a comprehensive step by step guideline to ensure that you climb to the social world hierarchy.

There you have it folks. Boxes 1 thru 19 have given you all a basic understanding of what is needed, and what you must do to be successful in the realm of internet marketing.

We invite you to join us in Boxes 20 thru 40. It is here that you will learn, in a formatted step by step process, how to engage all the necessary components of bringing your business to the next level.

Now Folks, it's time to go; we are burning daylight here. We have a job to do, and we will work hard at that job because "Your Success is Our Success." We believe it, we live it.

BOX 20

"YOU HAVE COME TO THE END, AND HAVE FOUND THE BEGINNING."

You had to make a decision to get here, and that for some of you may have been a very large commitment. Marty and I take your commitment as seriously as you do, and we, and our entire team, will do everything humanly possible to ensure that the decision you made to engage in IM is 100% correct.

Before we dive in, we want to outline what will be happening in all the subsequent boxes that you will be receiving:

In boxes 1 thru 19, you were given the overview of various applications and processes that will be necessary to develop and operate a successful on-line business.

Starting here, you will be receiving a very in-depth instruction, of not only the "how", but also of the "why."

What you have discovered and learned up to this point, and what you are about to learn and discover going forward, is sort of like the difference between the **"lightning bug and the lightning."**

As a result, each Box will be longer and much more detailed, so we recommend that you fully absorb Box 20, before proceeding to Box 21 and so forth, right up the line.

Let's go folks, we are burning daylight here!!!!!!

First, we are going to start with the most recent changes to the Google algorithms, known as Panda, Penguin and Hummingbird. The reason we are starting here is to make you well aware of not only where the web is now, but where it is going in the future.

Google, Yahoo, MSN, Bing and the host of smaller search engines are all aligning themselves away from a "keyword" ranked indexing system, and heading very rapidly to a "Consumer Connected" ranking system.

While keyword ranking will still play a big part of the equation, it will no longer count for up to 60% as it has in the past. We believe that, going forward, this factor will remain at around 25% of the total ranking equation. (Note: This is an educated guess.)

On the flip side of the coin, we believe that the "Consumer Connected" ranking factors, which most experts had put in the 05%-10% range, will climb in importance and take up 60+% of the ranking algorithm.

We might not predict the numbers *exactly*, but the direction is crystal clear. This is not an educated guess, or a wish, or a dream; this is what is going to happen, and you are getting an insight into the future.

The good thing about it is that the professionals that are driving the search engine results right now, "the big players", are slow to adapt to change. At this point, November 2015, about 90% of the websites and marketing campaigns out there are lagging behind in the consumer marketplace.

The corporate mentality says "if it isn't broke, don't fix it."

This is where you can get the upper hand in the near and distant future.

You have already started on the path of building a significant Social Media base. By the time the corporate social media technicians get around to changing their SEO strategies they will be way behind the curve.

Statistics surveyed (Smart Company Magazine) as of February 2011, show that only 43% of all major companies in the USA have actual budgeted social media programs.50% of those programs are destined for failure. Fast forward to 2015, these numbers have likely increased significantly.

This gives you a HUGE opportunity to brand yourself as a social media strategist and create another income stream (more on that in a later box).

Now that you understand that Social Media has to be employed in order to gain the page rank you need, let's take a look at a few of the vehicles that we will utilize to get us there:

Dropjack.com
Fark.com
Tumblr.com
Twicsy.com
Business-planet.net
Myspace.com
Multiply.com
Blogger.com
sitepronews.com/
Tumblr.com

Business-planet.net
Reddit.com
Stumbleupon.com
Google.com/Bookmarks
Technorati.com
Slashdot.org
Diigo.com
Wirefan.com
Twitter.com
Megite.com/discover/
Facebook.com

Of course, this is not a complete list and you will get more in future boxes. However, this list is a great starting point for you to integrate your social media campaign. The reason for this list is so you can begin to measure and optimize how you share.

To reach the largest audience, you need to be able to measure what works and what doesn't work, as you would with any marketing analytics. Then you can use your findings to fine-tune your efforts.

You can start by tracking your click-through rate by using bit.ly to create any links used to publish.

How does bit.ly work?

Bit.ly works by issuing a "301 redirect": a technique for making a webpage available under many URL's.

When you shorten a link with bit.ly, you are redirecting a click from bit.ly to the destination URL. A 301 redirect is the most efficient and search engine-friendly method for webpage redirection, and this is what Bit.ly uses. Since bit.ly doesn't re-use or modify links, it considers all redirects to be permanent.

This will enable you to determine which specific posts that you have published get a click through to your main site. (Remember to never send a new contact to a sales page.)

Start spreadsheet tracking for the social sites above that you choose to use using bit.ly links. The sidebar on your bit.ly account will give you the number of people that clicked on your redirect and you'll be able to distinguish exactly where that person clicked from.

They are always redirected to your main page, where you begin the sales funnel process, and after you have established a connection to them.

This exercise likely makes you aware of the importance of segmenting your spreadsheet lists of all the sites you are participating in into categories.

If you are anything like most of the people who use Twitter and Facebook, your Followers and friends have no focus.

They are just a random collection of names, and most of them have no interest in what you are doing. This situation needs to be corrected in order for your social media campaign to be effective.

It would be much better to have 300 targeted friends/followers, than 3000 random ones. 300 targeted leads will have a conversion rate 10 times that of 2000 random leads. Believe it!

Develop and Launch your Strategic Plan NOW.

To get you started on your strategy, always plan to include in your Tweets, Comments and Posts **"your keywords and/or keyword phrases"**.

How this simple part of a strategy has eluded so many so-called professionals never ceases to amaze us. Google has all but stood on their roof and yelled that they were indexing social media. Well, what do you think they are indexing? Yep, keywords.

Make a Notepad list of your keywords and key-phrases, so that you can copy and paste them into your tweets and posts and shares. Always have your link inserted to any Tweets, Posts and Shares, with an intelligent comment.

A few of the free tools that you will be using to formulate your plan will be www. twitalyzer.com, www.klout.com, www.tweepi.com, www. twellow.com

Example from Rich:

> *I went to tweepi.com and entered into their Twitter search section. I was looking for people interested in Parrots, it gave me 30 results. Now, the first 2 on the list was for a non-profit "Avery Organization" and the second one was a man that operates a Parrot Fanciers Club.*

> *More importantly, they had 3087 followers between them. When I clicked on their list of followers, there were literally hundreds of people who were connected to Parrots in one shape or form. This was "list mining" at its best.*

> *Here is also where this list mining has a two-fold purpose. As I reviewed the lists of these 2 frontrunners, I found 406 followers with a link to "join" them on Facebook.*

> *I followed the link, requested a friend and added a personalized note that I was involved in teaching parrots to talk, and left a bit.ly link to my article. (Make a note on Notepad, and all you have to do is enter their name before you copy and paste).*

Now I was building my Facebook friends list, with targeted prospects, as well as building my Twitter list.

Every time you write an article, or post to your blog, it is imperative that you have a Facebook "like" button, a "tweet this" button, and a "share this" button attached to the end of your article. Always include the note "I would really appreciate it if you shared my post with people whom are interested in our subject."

This is what will make your brand go viral. You build your fan page on Facebook based on your niche.

For example, we have built the fan page called "Polly's Parrot World". An admin surfs the net and uploads pictures of Parrots and links to videos on YouTube to fill the pages with content that would be of interest to those people in the Parrot Niche.

As the targeted lists develop, herein lays your opportunity to establish your authority and brand.

Remember, we have taught you to never sell anything directly from Twitter and Facebook or LinkedIn, these platforms are for establishing yourself as an authority, and for delivering valuable content.

Later, down the sales funnel is where you direct people to your landing page through your article or blog or link.

The main goal here is to keep directing people to your money page (main site). This is where you will earn revenue from Google Ads and from your affiliate links, even if the prospect does not buy directly from you at this time.

At the same time, you are also building your other important asset, your "email" list. In Box 27 we go through a full tutorial on the 7 steps to a successful email marketing campaign.

There is a lot more that we will be covering in the social media arena. For now, you have a lot of setup work to do, so we would like to pause here and give you the time to think through your strategy and set up your additional social media accounts.

You will notice on our main site, the "I would like to know" section. You can post questions or problems here and get your answers. This section is open format, and anyone can post a question and post an answer. Our staff will monitor the "answer" section just to ensure that no erroneous information is posted.

Folks, we will see you in Box 21 shortly, and thanks for letting us be part of your life. We appreciate it; we thrive in it.

Rich and Marty.

BOX 21

TWENTY GROUP COLLABORATIVE INTERNET MARKETING TRAINING

I've Got Rhythm,

I've Got Rhythm,

Who can ask for anything More. ?

RICHARD MCKELVEY & MARTIN SAPOSNICK

W hen George Gershwin wrote the words to his timeless song, I doubt very much that he had Internet Marketing Training and Twenty Group participation in mind.

As Dorothy said to Toto, "I don't think we are in Kansas anymore".

Now we are 80 years into the future, and one thing still holds true. You need to develop rhythm.

You will now discover the first of the "Five Golden Keys" in internet marketing: RHYTHM

We all look for the so-called "magic bullet" that will catapult us to success overnight. Well, you can stop looking now. There is no magic bullet, or secret button, or amazing new system that will earn you $127,531.77 in the next 5 days. However, there is something much more powerful, much more sustaining than any illusionary magic bullet you can find, or someone tries to sell you.

What exactly is the "Rhythm" Golden Key?

It is consistency, focus and discipline.

Building a Internet Marketing Business is all about getting your message in front of eyeballs. You cannot just go haphazardly about building a website, doing a halfhearted job of optimizing the site, and the sending out a tweet or shout-out or an article here and there.

RHYTHM is the systemic building of your social communication that needs to become an integral part of your marketing plan. (see Golden Key # 2).

The good news about Rhythm is that once you have set it up, you can delegate this task to your admin, or use one of the automated services that are explained in the resource box in the addendums.

The essence of Rhythm is that you must set up a consistent schedule to get your message out. It will not be enough to send out a tweet once or twice a day; it will never get to your market.

Remember, Twitter and Facebook and LinkedIn, etc., are in real time. Pretty much any blurb that you send out has a life span of a New York minute.

Everything that you setup must have only one purpose, and that is to drive your prospects to your money page.

The way to do that is through consistency. Your target market NEEDS to get used to seeing you over a long time span.

They NEED to see that you are directing them to relevant important content. They NEED to see that associating with you is beneficial to THEM. If it is also fun to associate with you, so much the better. In other words, YOU need them to keep YOU in the top of their minds.

One of the tactics that is simple to set up is to go to www.Quora.com and set up an account that corresponds to your account on Facebook (same brand).

Understand that Quora literally has thousands of questions, and answers. One of the best ways to engage prospects in your niche is to post questions through Quora and onto Facebook. When prospects in your target market niche see a question that they have been having an issue with, you can bet that they will click on the link to see what solution you have for their problem.

Naturally, when you provide answer on Quora, you will have the link to your website, where they will need to go to find further information on the subject.

This is a very effective tactic to drive unique visitors to your website, and keep them engaged with your opt-in offers.

This is the start of the viral effect. You must place the Facebook "like" button at the end of any problem solving issue that you post on Quora, and don't be shy about asking the reader to "like" your comments. When you do this, and the person hits the "like" button, it goes to every person on his friend list on Facebook.

How simple is that? If a person has 250 friends on Facebook, reads your comment, and "likes" it, then 250 other people see it. The number gets even larger if they like it also, because it goes to their friends. So, in effect, your message has the possibility to be seen by thousands of people that you have had no direct contact with.

Likewise, you want to create an article based on the question and answer, and post it on Google+ or Bing.com, and send the link over to Facebook, Twitter, and Linkedin.com.

Always title the article on "How I solved the problem of". (insert the niche problem) ... Example: "How I solved the problem of my parrot cursing" or "How I got my Facebook Fanpage to work properly" or "How I solved sleep apnea". You should be getting the idea at this point.

People NEED to solve problems, since that is how you engage them. If you are not an expert on the particular set of problems within your niche, either become the expert or reference a credible expert that has reliable answers.

This is where we come back to RHYTHM, you need to set up a schedule to allow the time to complete this process. This can be set up automatically on Tweepi and a dozen other sites that complete this automation for you. Or the more advanced systems that we advise and direct our multi-website users to utilize.

Example:

Post from Anywhere » To Anywhere

Our Twenty Group students will recognize the above logo belonging to PING.fm, and we used it in conjunction with Hootsuite.com. This allows you to integrate up to 41 social media sites and your blog.

Setting It All Up:

First, log into your Hootsuite account.

Connect your blog's RSS Feed

Next, you want Hootsuite to send your blog posts automatically every time you post. To do this, click on the RSS/Atom tab in Hootsuite.

Just add your blog's RSS feed and select the services you want it to automatically post to.

Post from Anywhere » To Anywhere

WOW, we just turned several days of work into about 2 hours, and now you have syndicated YOURSELF.

In Box 20, we gave you a list of Social Media sites that you may want to consider to add to your personal syndicate. We go much more in-depth on this process at the IVD (internetvisionsdefined.com) site in the resource area of the site.

Along with our complete tutorial for our more advanced students, you will learn how to segment all your social media sites.

So, as you start your RHYTHM phase, don't attempt to do too much at one time: look, study and learn. Above all, ask us the questions you are not sure of, and we will get the answers to you...WHO KNOWS, it might make a great engagement question on Quora.

OK folks, that's enough for today. We are burning daylight here, and you have a ton of work to set up.

Remember, on the internet you have 7 seconds to capture their attention.

See you on the other side of Box 22.

Rich and Marty

BOX 22

MAKING YOUR BUSINESS A "DESTINATION"

Do you believe that the above brands are Social Media Sites?

Do you believe you are in the Internet Marketing Business?

If you answered "NO" to the above 2 questions, you are 100% correct You will find out all about the above in a moment, but first let us talk about one simple fact concerning the 96% failure rate of our industry. That is: most business people just don't not understand what the "Internet Business" really is all about.

We're not saying that they don't understand all the basic technical aspects. They know about building a site, and some vague idea of SEO. They may also know about autoresponders and building a list. They have been told that they need to be socially engaged, but don't know exactly what that means. They have skills, but can't figure out how or where to apply them. All of this is because they don't know what type of business they are in.

They simply just couldn't find this.

The reason they couldn't find their magic button, is because they were looking in the wrong place.

They were looking for it in the "Internet Marketing Business", exactly where it does not exist.

It only exists in our "real and true" industry............

You can bet your bottom dollar that this is our business.

With our "Show Business" we mix in a little of this:

Give your target audience a good show, add in a little suspense of things to come, and you have now learned "the secret". With the realization that you are not in the "selling things on the internet" business, commonly known as the "Internet Marketing Business" you can get down to the real part of what we do.

Now you can have fun and enjoy the business, because you now know what you do. We can now get back to the tasks of building our show business productions.

Golden Key # 2

Production Marketing Plan.

As we referenced in Box1, Golden Key #1, Rhythm, goes hand in hand with PMP (Production Marketing Plan).

All of our marketing plans have only one purpose and one direction. It is our sole purpose to drive traffic to our website, where it is our job to convert.

The conversion process has many steps, and they are all sequential. We will explore that area of our marketing process in a little while, but first we want to make sure that we have the actual marketing process down to a science first.

Attract + Persuade + Convert = Success

The above 3 steps are complete tutorials within themselves, so we will explore and explain each one individually.

1). Attract: Up to this point, you have been setting up all your social media platforms, and adding content without the sales funnel. Now it is time to attract your target market to your website, where the sales process begins.

2). Here is where your newly developed skills as a copywriter will come into play. You need to make your headlines compelling enough so that members of your target market will want to respond to your "call to action".

3). Always start your headlines with a question:

> Do you need to know_____.?
> Would you like to discover the secrets to_____.?
> Would you like to learn the 4 steps necessary
> to succeed _____.?

Do you see the point here; you have taken "I" out of the equation. Never use a phrase that begins with "I", because most people will recognize that word as a benefit to "you" and not to them.

You need to present a solution to **Their** problem.

4). Be proactive in your own content distribution. You cannot be shy about this. Ask your audience to pass along the information to their friends, fellow tweeters, or their followers. Ask them for comments, by saying, "I would appreciate the favor of a comment, if you liked the information". This is very important in making your content go viral.

5). The "attract" process needs to be relentless, you need to employ all your distribution sites. (see mind-map 22-1 on our website). This needs to be done repetitively during your initial launch period. The whole idea is to keep the content fresh with redistribution through the viral network. This is the essence of Network Marketing.

Do not start your "Attract" process before you have all your tools in place. Your "Attract" campaign must have all the "follow through" information ready and available.

When someone is "attracted" to your page, they need to find their call to action, which is your opt-in box. This is the whole purpose of what you are doing. At this point your autoresponder needs to do its work.

You have to have this process set up to respond to your prospective client by delivering the content that you have promised. You need to test this on yourself before you send it out, to make sure that the proper information is delivered as you want, and in a timely manner.

Let us go over an example:

You prepare the information article that you want to draw your readers to, and you publish this on your Wordpress.org Blog. (This will become your "base" for the time being).

1). You will also have a hyperlink on your website pointing to your blog (but we will go into more detail on that in a later box).
2). Name your blog for the "keywords" you want to target. Example: Teach your "Parrot to Talk" in 24 hours.
3). Embed photos and videos into your blog. In the "Attract" process you need to engage your target audience. **DO NOT SELL**.
4). Make sure that the call to action on your blog is to "subscribe". In this way you are now creating a segmented list.

The first list were the people that wanted to read your article and move on. The second list is the people who have now given you permission to "engage" them.

Both lists are important. The first list you will continue with the engagement process, and the second list you will start the sales process. The goal here is to "Attract" as many of the first list prospects as possible onto the second list.

The second tier of "Attract" is content distribution. You need to get your "attraction generator in front of eyeballs. This is why it was pointed out in previous boxes that it is of vital importance to create and maintain your "systemic channel of content distribution".

This needs to be automated. It is hard enough to spend the time creating your content; you just cannot afford to spend time to distribute and post to every one of your social media sites one at a time.

Remember, Hootsuite was recommended to get this task accomplished. Hootsuite costs under $10.00 a month, and it is well worth the investment.

While you are building your Attraction social media campaign, do not just stick to the obvious LinkedIn for your business contacts. Have your admin constantly working on the secondary business connection sites.

Niche Social-Media Sites

Consider linking up with one of these social-media sites to narrow down your business's target audience.

Pixel Groovy: Web workers will love Pixel Groovy, an open-source site that lets members submit and rate tutorials for Web 2.0, email and online-marketing issues.

Mixx: Mixx prides itself on being "your link to the Web content that really matters." Submit and rate stories, photos and news to drive traffic to your own site.

Tweako: Gadget-minded computer geeks can network with each other on Tweako. (Keeps you up to date on trending topics in the IT world).

Small Business Brief: When members post entrepreneur-related articles, a photo and a link to their profile appear, gaining you valuable exposure and legitimacy online.

Sphinn: Sphinn, now Marketingland.com is an online forum and networking site for the Internet marketing crowd. Upload articles and guides from your blog to create interest in your own company or connect with other professionals for form new contacts.

"Always believe you are not the smartest guy in the room and let other people bring ideas to the table," says Marty. The path you start for your business – and often your endpoint as well – will change drastically as you build the company.

BuzzFlash.net: This one-stop news resource is great for businesses that want to contribute articles on a variety of subjects, from the environment to politics to health.

Do not make your Attraction Marketing half a job, remember the old saying "I have places to go, people to meet, and obligations to keep". Do it right.

When you do, we will see you on the other side of Box 23 to continue.

Rich & Marty

BOX 23

PERSUADE

EDUCATE, ENGAGE, EMPOWER & CONNECT

We used the social web to attract visitors, as we outlined in Box22. We must now also use these same sources to distribute our persuasion content.

At this point we wish to go back and refer to Box1. In step 4 of Box 1, we have stated that you need a clear and concise idea of who your target market is going to be.

Now you will see the importance of why you needed to do that. After the attraction process has begun, you need to convince and persuade your target audience that there's real value included in the information and guidance that you provide.

You have selected your target niche because you are the expert on the subject that is of most importance to the entire niche.

(The statement that YOU selected your target niche is an oxymoron). YOU didn't select the niche; the target market selected the niche for YOU. This is because of their related searches on the internet.

When you begin your persuasion process, you need to reverse your thinking process and put yourself in your target markets shoes. Why have they come to you? What are they seeking?

It is simple; they are looking and seeking because:

They have a Problem

They face a Challenge.

They have a Fear

Or they have a Desire.

Consequently, your persuasion process will be 4 pointed.

You will not be sending out the same messages to your target market via the social media, and the "unsociable" media (email).

You will be targeting each of the above points separately. So let's break out our persuasion points (examples):

On Facebook you send out a short status report: I had a huge problem teaching my parrot how to talk until I watched this 3-minute video.... bit. ly xxxxxx. (A blurb like this on Facebook and Twitter is solely designed to pique the interest of all the readers who are involved in this niche.)

This bit.ly takes them to your VERY simple landing (lead capture) page.

You have a short bio about your parrot and a cute picture of yourself with your parrot.

The opt-in box on your landing page lets your target market enter their email address to get access to the 3-minute video; asking them where to send the video usually does it.

Now of course, you have to make this 3-minute video, (which you will learn in Box 30), and it has to deliver much more than you promised. It needs to solve their immediate Problem.

Once you have done this, you have created a "fan". You have established yourself as the "authority" on your subject. You didn't try to sell them anything; you just did them a big favor.

After you have solved their immediate problem, you put a teaser at the end of the video, i. e., "after you have followed my instruction on how to teach your parrot how to talk, stop by my blog and I will show you how I taught my parrot to sing in only 2 days.

On the bottom of the video page you will have a comment box, a "like" button, a "share" button and, most important, an invitation to subscribe to your blog. The whole purpose here is to create the circle of continuity.

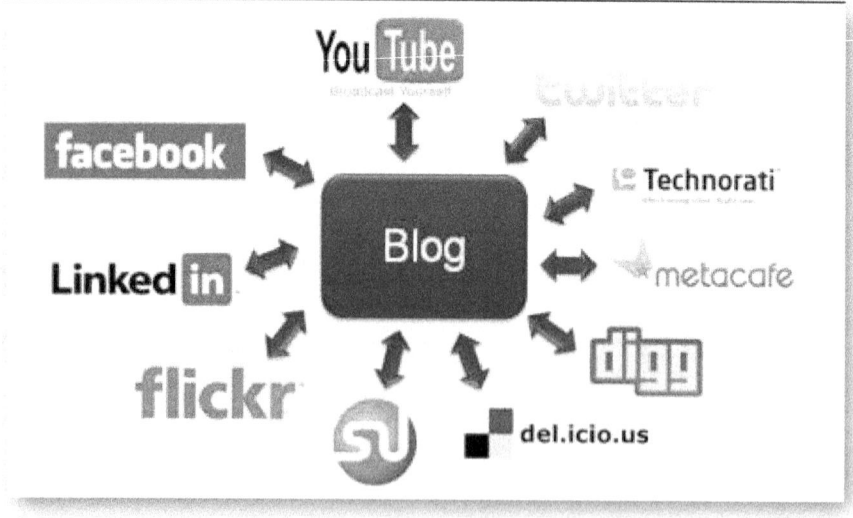

The persuasion process is intended to keep your target market engaged. It is not a one-way pitch; the information process gives them a feeling of comfort, so keep it genuine.

When you are engaging your audience, you are only giving statements that result in a "yes" answer.

In the page below, you will find a list of 15 important guidelines for you to follow through the persuasion process. Copy and paste it to your notepad, print it, and keep it where you can see it, as you design your persuasion campaign.

1. Use a bigger font size for your content.
2. Always use a squeeze page for capturing leads.
3. Optimize your "above the fold" to capture people with short attention spans.
4. Write with wise words that attract readers to read everything you have to say.
5. Always offer freebies as a "bribe" for capturing leads.
6. Remove the Name field from your opt-in box for higher conversions.
7. Change the Submit button to something more appealing.
8. Apply the "less is more" concept to your work.
9. Don't cloak links or use reverse psychology to get sales.
10. Introduce yourself to the customers, with a photo.
11. Tell your personal experience with the product you're promoting.
12. Display quality testimonials and invite new customer testimonials too.
13. Talk in a friendly and casual manner, and don't use difficult academic words.
14. Blend your content with images and decorative designs.
15. Get straight to the fact and let your readers know what you are about...... then sell.

How do we sum up the persuasion process, well, one of my mentors, Brian Tracy, made a memorable statement at a seminar attended many years ago that still applies:

"Between you and every goal that you wish to achieve, there is a series of obstacles and the bigger the goal, the bigger the obstacles. Your decision to be, have, and do something out of the ordinary entails facing difficulties and challenges that are out of the ordinary as well."

"Sometimes your greatest asset is simply your ability to stay with it longer than anyone else."

This can be translated to mean "If it was easy, everybody would be doing it"

The purpose of Box 23 is to get you thinking "Inside the Boxes", while beginning the process of persuasion on yourself.

You are the "expert", so start thinking like one. We believe you have enough "food" for thought today, so let's get going on putting your persuasion process together. We are burning daylight here.

In Box 24, the "Conversion Box" and the completion of this 3-part process, we would like to show you the top 10 email headlines that will boost your "open" rate to 10 times the industry standard.

So, stop getting ready to get ready, and we will see you on the other side of Box 24.

Rich and Marty

BOX 24

CONVERSION

N ow that you have gone through your Attraction and Persuasion
processes, you are ready to convert your audience to **BUYERS**.
From the time you started your internet marketing on day one, where
we explained how important it is to know who your target market is;
you should have been forming in your mind what your end product
would be. (You can expand on this later as we have a complete tutorial on Product Creation in Box28).

At the end of the conversion module, you will be able to recognize
the #1 source of sales generation on the internet today, but first let us
step you through the initial sale and the up-sell sales pyramid.

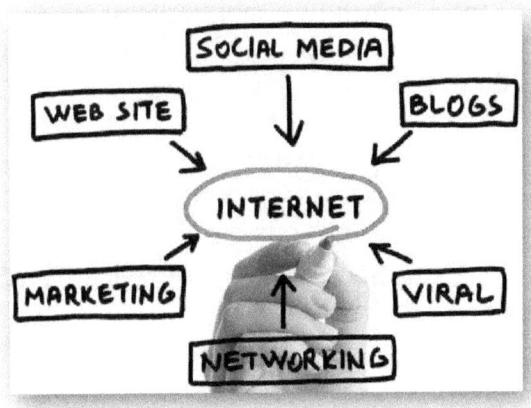

By now you have built a relationship with your list through your series of free content delivery, they are primed and ready to purchase from you. All you have to do is ASK.

Since you have established yourself as one of the top experts in the virtual "Parrot World", it would be a simple task to offer for sale a 1 or 2-disc video tutoring lesson on the "Art of Training Parrots".

Understand that to reproduce a 2-disc video set it will cost about $1.10, and the mailer from the US Post Office is $.78 cents. So for about a buck ninety you have a product to launch. Or, you can offer it as a download and allow them to burn a copy to their own discs; your cost is $0.00.

Now at the base level of your sales pyramid, you want to price a product at $9.97.

Wow you say to yourself, I can make a whole 7 bucks a sale, or $9.97. Hang on a minute, while I go out and place an order for my yacht!

Well, the point is that you will never make any real money from the bottom of your pyramid; that is not the purpose.

The whole purpose is to produce a high quality product that delivers tremendous value to your target market. Then when you get to the next offer, you do not have to persuade or convert.

You already own the market, and they will purchase from you, without question, without hesitation.

So, when you move up the pyramid, the next price point would be within the $24.97 to $47.97 range.

As the price point escalates 3 to 5 times the original offer, so does the profit point escalate 3 to 5 times.

Now, let us look at the low end of the pyramid. If you only make 2 sales a day, for a 3-month period, you would yield a profit of about $630.00. O.K., agreed, no yachts yet.

Then you go to the second level and repeat the same sales, and now you yield a profit of about $3,150.00. (Still no yacht yet, but that rowboat is starting to look sweet).

Understand that even with the bare minimum of sales, you can start to see the formation of a real life company being born.

The company that YOU are building will take on a life of its own sustainability. An effective tactic to use is through an autoresponder. (An autoresponder is a program that automatically generates a set response to all messages sent to a particular email address.) After the initial sale, the first follow up email is to thank our clients, let them know how much they are appreciated for their purchase. Always include a populated comment box so that they can tweet or share or tumble or whatever. ASK them for a favor and send it.

Also reinforce that if they are not 100% satisfied, they can have their money refunded. Make sure that they know that if they have any questions, they could send an email, and get a personal reply.

Now is the time we want you to start thinking about your customer service, because this is what will set you apart in your niche.

Do not think of yourself as an Internet Marketer with great customer service. We want you to think of yourself as a "Great Customer Service Company", who happens to be involved in Internet Marketing.

This is your playing field:

The Internet

It has no limits.

An Example from Rich:

In this moment, I would like to recount a personal story and how I became a subject of conversion. (Of course I didn't know this until years later).

Early in my business career, way before the personal development movement became popular; I read a book called "The Science of Personal Achievement" by Napoleon Hill.

Please keep in mind that this was back in 1967, before the internet. Anyway, I thought this book was very insightful, and I sought out other books by the author. About two years later, I noticed an ad in a local newspaper that offered this same book on a tape cassette selling for $3.95.

You clipped the coupon, filled it out and mailed them a check for the purchase. (Credit card purchases were not that big yet).

Ten days later I received my cassette, which was narrated by a man named Earl Nightingale.

These generally sold in the $14.95 to $29.95 range, remember this was a while ago. I purchased a few of these "training programs," and I was always pleased with the product. Without ever knowing it, I was in their sales pyramid.

Over the next several years I purchased products ranging from $99.00 to $299.00, without ever having regret.

Do you see the parallel here, they first sold me a set of six to eight cassettes for $29.95 and graduated me, over a period of time, to the next level of six to eight cassette sets for $299.00

The process was painless for me, and they were reaping 10 times the initial sale, at the same production cost. To top it all off, they had created a lifelong repeat customer, as I still purchase from them today.

All in all, I have probably spent 10 thousand dollars, over a thirty-year period with them. One customer, starting at $3.95, has helped them grow into a billion-dollar company today.

I enjoyed every purchase and even made some friends along the way. I said at the beginning of this Box24 that I would show you the #1 source of sales generation on the internet today. Well, you are going to get a bonus, because there are 2 equally effective high conversion vehicles for you to use.

First, set up your own affiliate network. Wow, did that frighten anyone. It should not have, not at this stage of your learning curve. Just think for a moment and do the math. Today, there are close to 100,000 affiliate marketers registered on Clickbank.

They are all hungry, and they are looking for the next hot ticket item so they can keep their commissions rolling in. And you are here to help them.

Let's look at the numbers for a minute:

Say that you pick up a conservative 400 affiliate marketers, which is really an easy task, and each one of these marketers sells only a dozen of your products a month.

Well, that translates to 4,800 units a month. The "run life" of a product is usually about 90 days before it powers down.

At that rate, you will have sold 14,400 units of your product. Now, in order to motivate the affiliate sales force, you are going to have to pay up to about 70% commission.

Heck, you say, that is way too much.!!!!! Well, in reality, it is not. Because you are going to the affiliate market after you have a close-out sale to your list at $9.97.

You inform your list that the product will stop selling on a certain date and time, like 12 o'clock midnight on June 23, 2016.

When that is completed, you move the same product over to the affiliate market, at a sales price of $16.97. So, you net profit on each sale would be $5.08. or $73,152.00 profit on the 14,400 units sold.

Plus, the residual sales that go beyond 90 days. I say net profit because on each sale that is not downloaded, there is a $1.88 shipping and handling charge. (Gee, where did that exact figure come from).

Not wishing to sound puffy, these are very real numbers to achieve.

We will show you how in our "Goal Setter" tutorial in Box34.

However, this is not where the real value comes from. It comes from the fact, that the affiliate salespeople are sending the buyers to **Your** sales page to complete the transaction, and these buyers now become **Your** list.

Wow, you just became the benefactor of 14,400 people who have bought from **You**.

People who want to buy more stuff for their beloved parrots. Or maybe they even want to buy another parrot or two, and you, of course, have your partnership is set up with one of the biggest and best parrot sellers in the world. Are you beginning to see why there was a big blue circle in Box 23?

Now, the second greatest source for generating sales on the internet is within your own Twenty Group.

Nothing is sweeter than having 19 dedicated like-minded professionals selling your stuff. The only drawback is that they keep their own list; you don't get to share. On the plus side, you only pay a 40-50% commission to your peer group.

But you have a lot more fun within your group, by creating competition through a bonus plan. Now if you believe that creating your own affiliate program is a little beyond your capability, do not fear. In Box 37 we have created a step by step tutorial for owning and operating your own network, and Marty is one of the leading experts in the country on forming and profitably operating affiliate networks.

So folks, our day comes to a close. You have a lot of thinking to do, a fair amount of work ahead, and we are burning daylight here.

So, we will see you on the other side of Box 25 with a few surprises that will make your internet marketing day a little brighter.

BOX 25

Please Exit "Listen Only Mode"

You have the workable knowledge, there are no secrets here.

We have selected this mid-way point in the "Internet Marketing Defined" series to teach you how to put all the previous knowledge you have gathered to work for you.

It is now time to start monetizing some of your efforts. As it is with a lot of things on the internet, people get confused as where to start because "they can't see the forest, and there are too many trees in the way". We have stated in previous boxes, that one of the easiest ways to earn on the internet is through affiliate programs.

Our goal here is not to teach you how to become an affiliate. Our goal is to turn you into a Super Affiliate. As stated before: the difference between an affiliate and a super affiliate is the same as the difference between the lightning bug, and the lightning.

The difference in income is several thousand dollars a year, versus several hundred thousand dollars a year. **The only barrier between the two is your mindset and your goals.** (We have a whole tutorial dedicated to the "Internet Mindset and Goal Achievement") in a later addendum and also available on our website.

The underlying reason for teaching you to become a super affiliate at this point in "your" learning curve, is to allow you to earn money in order to go on to your own success. You see, everything you have learned up to this point has been free, and our information to you will continue to be free.

However, as you progress from here, there will be expenses that need to be met. As in any business, online or offline, there are certain tools that need to be purchased in order to advance and add enhancements to your business.

These tools may be as simple as AdWords or Facebook Ads, LinkedIn Ads, or as involved as automated programs that you will need to streamline your business efforts. Whatever the case may be, there will be costs involved, and it is our philosophy that these expenses are better met with earned money, rather than out of pocket costs. We are sure you will agree.

Let's start the process.

7.6 million Unique visitors a week

Just think of the possibilities.

First, if you do not have a regular consumer account on Amazom. com, go ahead and set yourself up there. Note: This is not absolutely necessary, but will be helpful later down the line. Once you go to the Amazon.com site, go to the bottom of the main page and find the tab that says "Affiliates". Fill out all the required information and submit your application, it usually takes 2-4 days for Amazon to review your site and approve your application. Now, here comes the interesting part
.

Amazon.com gives you all the tools for free, to build a website, add widgets, display products, create a check-out page and add shopping cart, it gives you banners and text links. It also recommends products for you based on your home website.

.

It allows your customers to search the entire Amazon.com catalog system with the link from your site, and it provides you with images and up to date pricing. WOW! How could you not be able to create your own cash cow with this type of support.

EXAMPLE:

When you start, and believe me, you can create your own Amazon. com "aStore" in less than 30minutes. Then you will be able to promote from your website, or stand-alone site. You name your site, as you wish, and this is how it will be displayed on Amazon.com. Is this exciting or what?

You have the technical support of the largest retailer in the world, and their only goal is to make sure that you are successful. Most people are unaware of how the system works, but Amazon.com is just the Mall. Therefore, all the sellers on Amazon.com are the Mall tenants, much like the stores in your local Mall, with the exception that you do not pay Amazon.com rent, like the brick and mortar stores do at the local mall.

You pay them a commission on the sales that you make through Amazon.com, from your affiliate links when you sell your own products, and visa-verse when you sell products from the affiliate catalog. Now, if you go back to Box23, and study the "Circle of Continuity" charts, you will see how this all comes into play. You can drive traffic to your "aStore" from your blog, or through your social media sites, or through links you post on your article marketing site, etc.etc.

Make sure always start by adding a top level "Store" section to your website's main navigation page.

You will want to make the links to your site with products that are relevant first, and **give them above the fold exposure.**

Example: If you are on your Parrot Training Blog, you will want to exhibit parrot vitamins, parrot toys, parrot environment products, and so forth. Then you can add to the mix by letting Amazon.com suggest products based on your blog theme or site content.

They have a widget plug-in that does this, and also rotates products for you. However, all the plug-ins that they offer you is not the **"Jewel"** of the system. The real power is that Amazon.com allows you to create up to 100 "aStores" on a single account. Just let that number "100" sink in for a little while.

THINK of all the possibilities that you as a marketer can do with all that fire power. You have the ability to set up "Review" sites with the "aStores" and literally market hundreds of products at the same time.

We show you how to refine the entire process in a future Box, but for now, if you feel you can't come up with more than a few products, the answer is easy, with research. Go over to the Amazon.com competition for a moment at http://pulse.ebay.com.

On this research tool, you can pull up the top 10 items searched on ebay.com, for the past week, in each and every category that ebay.com offers. How amazing is this. If you select only the top 4 products in each category, you can build and fill 100 "aStores" in a matter of a few days. Every week you can change items and products as the market demand changes also, because each "aStore' is fully customizable as you have full control over the "aStore".

You will want to create a mix of physical products and information products; this will ensure a continuous income stream from both sides of the aisle for months and even years to come. There are a few more sophisticated tactics that can be utilized to drive traffic to your "aStore", and we have a full tutorial on these tactics in a future Box.

At this time, you can get yourself up and running with as many "aStores" as you feel you can comfortably handle in the next 2 weeks. By the way, PLEASE don't tell me that you have created 5 "aStores", and you are ready for advanced marketing tactics. We didn't fall off the back of a pumpkin truck in New Jersey yesterday.

Put in your best efforts, think, and create, and we will be here to help you along the way.

So folks, you have enough work to carry you through the next several days. If you get stuck anywhere along this process, just drop us an email and we will send you over the solutions you need.

We will see you all on the other side of Box 26.

Rich and Marty

BOX 26

THE "ESSENCE"

We have elected to write Box 26 as the explanatory box, rather than a tutorial box, in order to keep everyone moving in the same direction.

In our industry it is quite easy to be distracted and lose our way, due to all the information we have been gathering.

So, we wanted to put the essence of what we do, back into focus, and to bring to the forefront the ideas and principles of what we do, in an easy to digest format.

Our Mission:

- **To be found online**
- **To convert visitors into leads and prospects**
- **To convert leads and prospects into paying customers.**

It does not get any simpler, or complicated than that folks.

This is not to be construed as a mission statement, it is only to explain what our current mission is. However, when you understand the current mission, you will begin to see how this can be replicated across multiple niches, and start to move you away from the single minded idea of what you originally wanted to sell via the internet. We do not want to deter you from your original sales ideas, we want you to realize and expand on them.

After many years of in-depth research and analysis, we have discovered the secret of becoming a successful sales entrepreneur in cyberspace:

Sell stuff people want.

Wow, what a revelation. We have also decided to share with you our basic fundamental principle that drives and motivates our business, and feel free to share our philosophy with anyone you wish to:

If it doesn't make money, it doesn't make sense.

Wow, a second revelation. In no way are the above two statements designed to be contrite. We state them with great emphasis in order to bring you back into focus. It is to give you a wakeup call that "your" idea of selling a great product or service may not be everyone's idea of what a great product or service should be.

In other words, don't get hung upon your original idea of how you will become successful.

Now, above we stated that the current mission is to be "found" on-line.

So with that, we create an action plan:

- Create a targeted landing page
- Include a CLEAR call to action
- Explain the benefit to the prospect
- Solve the prospects current problem

Once you have accomplished this part of the action plan, you now have the prospects permission for you to lead them down your sales funnel.

Keep in mind: People buy stories, not stuff.

Oh Great you say! All I have to do is to create a targeted landing page. No one has ever taught me how to do that. So now what? Well, let us go together and create a really great landing page.

The fundamentals:

In online marketing a landing page, sometimes known as a lead capture page, is a single webpage that appears in response to clicking on an offer that is of interest to the reader. The landing page will display directed sales copy that is a logical extension of the product or service that the reader is interested in.

Below are the 15 elements that are necessary for creating a successful Landing Page:

1. Have a dedicated Landing Page for each product or service.
2. Each Landing Page should connect and answer the search term.
3. Every Landing Page should have a clear "call to action" on the page.
4. Make Your Landing Pages as clean as possible with no links besides your "Call to Action".
5. Write Your Landing Pages in the First Person, like a direct letter to the reader.
6. Sign your name at the bottom - again, just like a letter.
7. Test and retest your Landing Pages.
8. Use a headline that directly connects to the search term.
9. Write in short paragraphs: 1-3 lines per paragraph.
10. Make your point in the first sentence of each paragraph.

11. Use some sort of Analytics to track your results.
12. Your Call to Action HAS to be measurable.
13. If your Call to Action is a form - make sure it's short.
14. Always end with a "thank you".
15. If possible, add your photo to the landing page.

OK, now you know what a landing page is, and what we teach you to put into it, let us proceed with building one.

But first, let's look at a few examples.

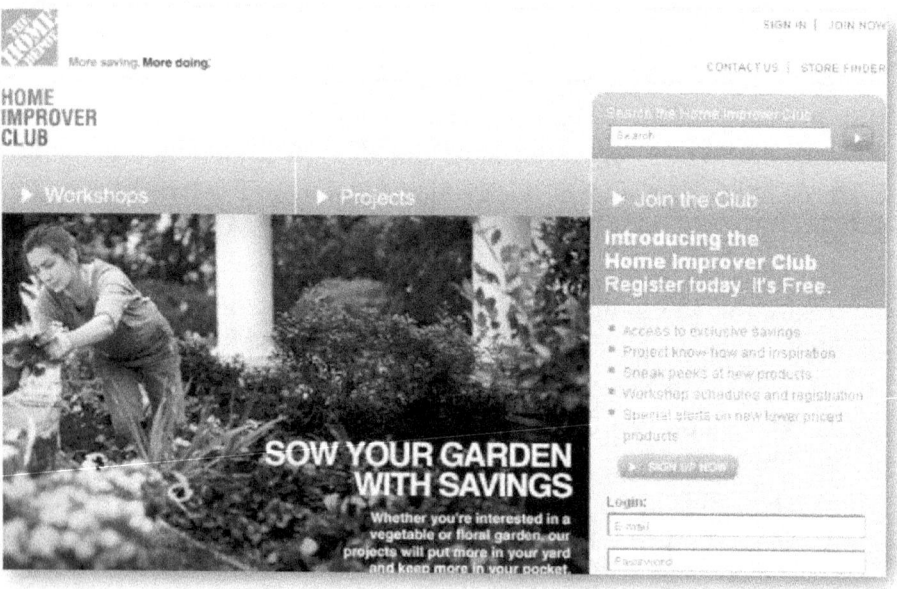

This, of course, is one form of landing page, designed not to look like a landing page. It is designed to look like a "join the club page". Make no mistake, it is a pure "landing page". It is solely designed to capture your name and email.

Now below is a landing page that targets the "newbies".

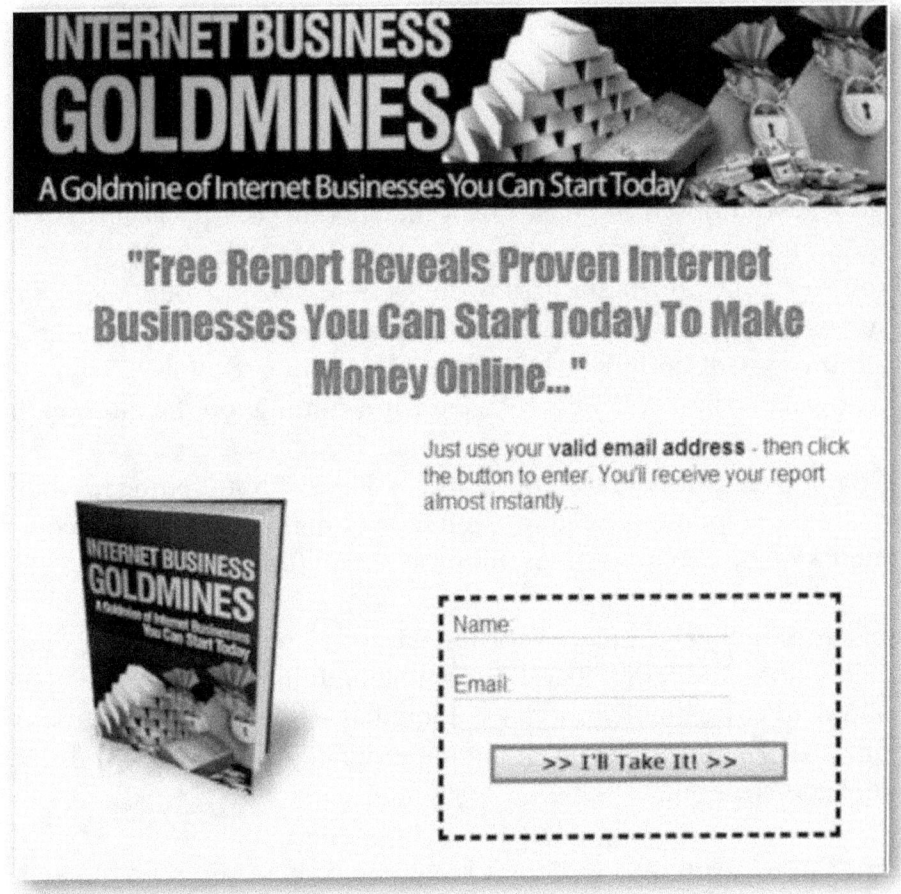

Now this image is exactly what it is representing itself to be. An email capture page. Unfortunately, the content is of such poor quality, really garbage that anyone above the 3rd grade would click-out immediately.

So, now you see, the first example is excellent, and the second example is pure trash. Now, one of the ways you can build your landing page, for those of you who are working with a WordPress blog is to install the opt-in widget that is available. However, it takes some technical skills to get it up and running correctly, so we do not recommend it for the technically challenged.

The best, and easiest way is to build a one-page website at GoDaddy or Hostgator, then go to your autoresponder, Aweber is recommended, and your opt-in response box is included in your package.

You just copy and paste it into the website you just built for your current campaign offer. The basic package costs less than 8 bucks a month on GoDaddy, which includes the hosting. So for 72 bucks a year you can have a Landing Page up and running on the internet.

Do not create and publish your Landing Page without setting up your complete response cycle in your autoresponder first. (We have a complete step by step tutorial on this process in a future box).

In contrast, there are some very popular social media publishing sites, called hubs and lenses where we can be building landing pages that allows us to customize the page content (text, images, anchor text links, alternate text for images, etc.), assign a title and even define a meta description.

For those of you who still don't know about these social media websites, let us introduce you to the world of hubs:

HubPages is very useful in terms of link building and content promotion; it offers a great ability to customize and optimize content.

Although it includes conversion and compensation mechanisms, many users use it strictly for SEO purposes.

If you want to sell a product or monetize it using AdSense, it can work well for both purposes. If you seek the SEO effect, it's also a great tool for link building.

There are four basic components of a successful landing page program:

Research
Design
Copy
Testing Modification.

It is important to devote adequate resources to each component they form a chain that is only as strong as the weakest link.

For instance, if you fail to properly research your audience, then the greatest design will never be able to save the campaign.

Similarly, a prospect might click away from copy that is too long or too short, regardless of how much research went into its development.

You will get a lot of insight on this in a future box, in the section we call the "Clever Truth". For now, we believe it is time to start your Landing Page experiments.

In the next box we will explore and define the process of "Architecting your Sales Conversion Process"

Until then, you have work to do, and we are burning daylight here. We will see you on the other side of Box27.

BOX 27

"The Value Exchange"

The concept above is quite simple and self-explanatory.
But, it is a concept that is often overlooked and misunderstood, especially in the internet marketing business.

You are asking your target market to exchange their time and contact information in order to receive something of value from you.

Think about that for a moment. As we have stated numerous times, the window of opportunity to capture their attention is about 7 seconds.

In this micro time frame, you must deliver a statement of value that will hold their attention, to captivate them, and to entice them to keep reading.

It is within this time frame that you must develop your skills as a copywriter.

Here are 14 tips that you need to understand as you develop your skill:

1. Aim for an average sentence length of 16 words or less.
2. Vary between short and long sentences to give your writing rhythm.
3. Split long sentences into two if they'll survive on their own. Use connecting words such as 'so', 'and' or 'because'.
4. Ask the reader a simple question early on that they will say 'yes' to. This will precondition them to be more likely to agree with you and say 'yes' to your offer later on.
5. Copywriting isn't blessed with a reader's patience. So ensure every word and sentence means something to the reader.
6. Leave long paragraphs to book writers, and limit each paragraph to a single thought. Four sentence paragraph maximum.
7. Showy writing isn't copywriting. Don't use words just because they sound impressive.
8. Only use positive inspiring language on what the reader 'can' achieve and 'will' be able to do.
9. Break up your page with subheads and bullets to aid skim reading.
10. Use power words to charge up your writing's impact, such as 'proven', 'scientific' and 'verified'.
11. Write in your reader's language and the style they're comfortable with. Read your target market's magazines and newspapers to gauge the pitch.
12. People are hardwired to respond to stories. Use storytelling on how your product has solved someone's problem to trigger the reader's imagination and emotions.
13. Use facts or personal history to build rapport, empathy and to show the reader that you feel their pain.
14. Copywriting is often compared to a conversation with a pal in a bar. So it should be conversational and sound similar to how you'd speak.

Make all your copywriting easier to read than to ignore. You have no human sales force, so something has to sell for you – and that something is words. Keep in mind that the first 20 words that you write, will count more than the 10,000 words that follow. Also keep in mind that you are "Only one great sales letter away from making a million dollars".

Wow, what a concept.

At this point we want to share with you the 10 proven 100% effective headline types that are necessary to build a copywriting campaign. We also want to make this tutorial a little interactive. We outline for you, 2 examples in each headline, and it is up to you to complete the next 3 examples under each heading.

1. The "Direct Statement" headline.
   Examples:
   a) The best cheesecake you ever ate. (Uncle Bill's Diner).
   b) 4 cents a minute anytime, 24-7, to anywhere in America!
   c)
   d)
   e)
2. The "Question" headline.
   Examples:
   a) Who else wants to know how to get massive traffic sent to their website?
   b) "Do you make these 4 basic mistakes on your first date?"
   c)
   d)
   e)

3. The "How-To" headline.
   Examples:
   a) How to optimize your website for maximum response.
   b) How to please your partner in bed quickly and easily.
   c)
   d)
   e)

4. The "Command" headline.
   Examples:
   a) This is your window of opportunity. Open it now!
   b) Enroll now and learn how to master tai-chi in just 90 days.
   c)
   d)
   e)

5. The "Implicit Benefit" headline.
   Examples:
   a) 7 sure-fire ways to maximize your profits on eBay.
   b) Change unsightly legs into Sexy legs in 5 minutes a day.
   c)
   d)
   e)

6. The "Guarantee" headline.
   Examples:
   a) "Double your website sales in one month or I'll pay you $500 cash!"
   b) The "Secret Science" that Guarantees to Make You a Better Negotiator.
   c)
   d)
   e)

7. The "Deep Discount" headline.
   Examples:
   a) "Buy 2 boxes of Pee-Poo pads today and receive 1 box free!"
   b) Get 4 "Triple XXX" rated full length DVD's for just $4 (Plus S&H).
   c)
   d)
   e)

8. The "Personalized" headline.
   Examples:
   a) "Marty, act fast... your special offer link expires in 48 hours on December 23"
   b) Finally, here's how you, Marty, can become an expert chef in 15 days.
   c)
   d)
   e)

9. The "Reasons Why" headline.
   Examples:
   a) Here are 7 money earning reasons to visit our website this week.
   b) 3 Invigorating Reasons Why Using 'Viagra' Will Make Your Life Easy!
   c)
   d)
   e)

10. The "Short, Punchy" headline.
    Examples:
    a) "What if..."
    b) "Oh My God!" (OMG)
    c)
    d)
    e)

Now, look back at your entries on lines c, d, e, and check to see if they contain any of the common "cockroach" words that we say will "Kill your Copy"

When writing headlines, subheads and body copy, don't use words that avoid a direct command, aka "cockroach" words.

These include: may, maybe, hope, wish, try, but, could, should, perhaps and strive. Instead, use words like WILL and CAN to describe what your product or service will or can do for your reader. Doing your own copywriting is not an easy task, but it is one that can be mastered with a little practice.

We advise that you do not look to professional copywriting services when you begin your first campaign. The reason for this is that no one can inject the passion for your product better than you, and, secondly, it is an expense that can be avoided with a little work.

Keep all of your copywriting focused in the same manner within all of your "points of contact" (touch-points) throughout the web. Potential customers within your niche like to see the same consistent flow to your thoughts and ideas.

We live in an increasingly web-savvy world in which people are accessing the web not only from their home computers, but also from their iPads, smartphones, laptops and more. Internet Marketers have the unprecedented opportunity to engage consumers at multiple touch-points throughout their day.

OK folks, you now have a little work to do in building your skills.

In Box28, you will learn how to select the proper URL's to coincide with your copywriting skills for your product or service.

You will be building, step by step, your first lead capture page so that you can drive traffic to your site and start producing revenue. You will learn to optimize the capture page and build links to it.

We are burning daylight here. It's time to stop getting ready to get ready, and we will see you all on the other side of Box28.

.

BOX 28

LANDING PAGE EMPIRE

I n Box27 we stated that we would begin the process of building a proper optimized landing page. And that we will do, but first let's go over a few notes.

In Box26 we gave you examples of the good and the not-so-good landing pages. It was our intent to get you to start your thinking process of how you want to protect yourself onto the world-wide-web.

One of the reasons is that, once you go live with a Landing Page, it is out there in cyberspace forever.

Even if you take down the page, the record always exists, and can be tracked down. Of course, most people do not have the ability to perform this function, (unless they have read "Internet Marketing Defined"), so the consequences may be small. However, you always want to keep this in mind.

Why did we title Box28 "Landing Page Empire"?

It is because we will not only instruct you how to build an effective landing page, but we will set you on the path to build and launch as many Landing Pages as your business heart desires.

We have a little over 30 Landing Pages working around the clock producing income. Granted, not every one of them is a home run. With 2 in the weight loss niche that produce about $5.00 per month, and 3 in the adult entertainment niche, about $150.00 per month for each is produced.

All the others, in many different niches, average about $30.00 to $55.00 per month. And since we've never met a dollar that we didn't like, Landing Pages that earn me $5.00 a month, are loved just as much as the ones that earn $150.00 a month.

In addition, there have been landing pages that have also earned $2,500 in a single month at least a dozen times on "hot button" niches. (We will go into these hot button niches a little later).
An example with Rich:

> *It does not matter how much or how little a Landing Page earns, because it will only take you about 20 minutes to create one. A single landing page can create income year after year. I estimate that I have earned a little over $1700.00 in the past 4 years on one of my Landing Pages about pimples.*

> *Yes, the common Zit, the plague of teenagers worldwide. I was just learning to create Landing Pages at that time, so it took me about 3 hours. So, by my figures, I earned $566.00 per hour, and counting, for my 3 hours of work. (I really hope they never find a "real" cure for pimples).*

Seriously though, the above statement always brings to mind, a quote from my mentor and friend:

> **"You don't get paid for the hour. You get paid for the value you bring to the hour".**
> **JIM ROHN**

Landing Pages when used properly, are added resources to your Internet Marketing business, and provide revenue streams that allow you to build your core business. As we have stated in previous Boxes, there will come a time that you will need to purchase certain tools to advance and increase your core business. This is the most excellent way to finance those necessary purchases.

Let's start: Most of you are familiar with Wix.com. They have great tools for building your one-page websites, and they are a great place to experiment and learn.

They are also for amateurs. We are building websites, as Landing Pages that we can optimize, for free, and publish on the web in about 20 minutes. We do this at Wix.com. Now for the purpose of this tutorial, Rich went to Wix.com, took his stopwatch, built this site, and had it published in 7 minutes and 35 seconds. www.wix.com/richardmckelvey/structure-for-success.

It has a total of 7 pages.4 of them main pages and 3 sub-pages. Of course it is very basic, what do you expect for 7 and a half minutes, the Mona Lisa?

Our purpose is to get you familiar with using Wix.com, and see how creative you can be. We named the site "Structure for Success", because that is what we will be doing in this and subsequent Boxes. We will teach you how to structure your Landing Pages, and show you how to link them to your points of contact to generate free traffic. (which of course is a misnomer that we explain a little later)

Now, Wix.com is not in the business of just providing free websites. As you build out your site, also take note of their business model. They are relentless, just the way you should learn to be. They are giving you something of true value, and, in exchange, they are given the opportunity to UPSELL you. This is a win-win situation.

You will most likely be purchasing one or two of their up-sell products... You most certainly will be buying the necessary URL once your site is perfected and ready to go live. Your investment will be less than 25 bucks per site...

Before you start building Landing Pages, you should understand the theory behind them, and then you will see how extremely necessary they are. (A point that is so misunderstood by internet marketers. It's a wonder what they are doing).

QUESTION: Why should you be using multiple landing pages instead of having the prospect go directly to your website?
ANSWER: TOUCHPOINTS. Explanation: You are promoting a product or service that will be searched for by people of all levels of different interests, various levels of expertise and education.

A single website cannot be optimized in order to reach everyone across these spectrums.

Assume that you have a website called "World of Parrots". Now, anyone who types those exact words into a search engine would be directed to your site. But if you were to type in "keeping my parrot healthy", you would be given a list of 10 million websites that contain the words "parrot" and "healthy".

So, you would be in competition with10million websites. Would they find you? It is not very likely to happen.

However, you have followed our tutorials in "Internet Marketing Defined", and have learned that by doing the proper Keyword research, you know that the top 10 searches for Parrots are:

- Training Parrots
- Teaching Parrots to talk.
- Vitamins for Parrots
- Singing Parrots

- Dancing Parrots
- Tattoos of Parrots.
- Types of Parrots
- Photographs of Parrots
- Cages for Parrots
- Raising Parrots for profit.

By looking at the above list, which represents about 85% of all the organic search concerning Parrots, how would you be able to optimize a single website in order to get 1st page place mention on Google? The only way of doing it, is by going to the Google headquarters in California and pull out a gun and threaten them with death if they didn't do it. Other than that scenario, you wouldn't have a clue.

BUT THERE IS A WAY TO DO IT:KEYWORD CONSTRUCTED LANDING PAGES.

Let us take the first search term on the list, Training Parrots. (We actually want you to perform this exercise).If you type in www.training-parrots.com, it will take you to a (parking) page, (which we explain in a future box) that shows you that this is not a real site, but it's the URL that is for sale for $1299.00.

Of course we are not buying this. We go to GoDaddy or HostGator or Wix.com, and we do a URL search. And then we find out that www. trainingparrots2.com is available with a cost of $8.99. (sort of makes you glad that you read this box).

Keep in mind that the suffix 2 we put on the end of the title name has no consequence when it comes to Google search.

We now create a Landing Page, with this title URL, and we optimize it with 25 variations of the Keywords that are relevant to training parrots. i.e. Training Parrots, Training Parrots to talk, Training Parrots in Spanish, Parrot Training Video, Parrot Training, parrots-parrots-parrots, so anyway, you get the message.

We are in Show Business folks, so what are we going to put on our Landing Page .... EXACTLY what Hollywood puts in a movie trailer commercial........ We now sell them the SIZZLE (not the steak) that prompts them to enter their name and email in order to be taken to our FREE Parrot Training Website.

When you see the movie trailer on your TV about a new movie to be released, they show you the best and most exciting clip. They are building your appetite to go and see the movie, where you will BUY a ticket, including several of their up-sells, like the $ 9.00 bucket of popcorn and the $4.50 cent cup of diet soda. Throw in a hot dog for $8.00 and your $10.00 movie ticket just cost you $ 31.50. And you didn't even notice.

Back to our training points. The Landing Page is also known as the Lead Capture Page, so it has 2 purposes and 2 very rewarding results.

The first purpose is to capture the prospects Name and Email; they then are made a part of our email master list. They will become part of our community. We will make them friends and have the ability to sell to them for months and years to come.

DO NOT take this lightly. The sales average for a customer on a niche targeted list is $130.77 over the life of the list.

Think of the numbers if you have 500, 1,000, 2,000 clients on a niche targeted list. Pretty impressive, and extremely profitable. The second purpose is to direct them to our main website, our money page.

Here is where we present our products or services, and allow them, with our expert guidance, purchase something additional from us.

Now you start seeing the real purpose of a Landing Page. No one, regardless of hard they try, can drive traffic to one website that will satisfy the needs of the top 10 searches in any niche.

WE CAN DO IT, however, by having 10 separate Landing Pages that are optimized for the target Keywords in each search term. And understand that all the Landing Pages are pointing to only one place, your main website.

This is the point where your foundation building on the Social Networks is going to pay off for you. We instructed you to build your following (community) centralized on one focal point. It makes no sense to have 5,000 followers or friends, if they are random.

It may have been dieting, health maintenance, dating, sexuality, self-improvement, physical training, beauty, etc., etc., etc..... It does not matter as long as you are targeting people of similar interests.

Now when you send out Tweets or post on Facebook or make a suggestion on Quora or wherever, and you say "I just found this great free video on training my Parrot", and you add your link to your text, the niche that you have been nurturing is going to reward you with a click thru.

When you make comments on a niche blog, and add your links, people are going to come and take a look at what you have to offer. After all, that is why they read the particular blog in the first place.

When they do this action, they are taken to your Landing Page. When they enter their information and click on the submit button, it takes them to your main website, where they get all the information they are looking for. And they can watch the videos and read the articles and get all kinds of great information and free stuff from you.

You have now reached the beginning of your sales funnel.

In Box29, we will instruct you on the complete cycle of monetizing your Landing Pages for additional income with ad placements and driving your clients to your affiliate partner commission generators.

Well Folks, we are burning daylight here, so why don't you pop over to Wix.com and start practicing. Get familiar with the formats that will become a big part of your success. See you all on the other side of Box29.

BOX 29

Landing Page Greatness in Seven Steps.

**Formal education will make you a living;
self-education will make you a fortune.**
"Jim Rohn"

Y ou just read the Jim Rohn quote above. Did you understand its meaning?

We provide you with all the tools, blueprints and processes necessary to become successful in all the boxes you have read, and will read going forward, but unless you take action and work at it, nothing will happen.

Creating a powerful Landing Page is the most critically important step in the sales funnel process. Give it the priority it needs and deserves.

Step 1:

Have a clear and concise call to action.

When you start your campaign, you only have one goal, and one opportunity to capture the interest of your audience.

This is what your Landing Page NEEDS to do.

Let your prospective client know exactly what they need to do in order to receive the item of value that you have offered. Set your "opt-in box" in the most prominent place on the page.

Fill out the form below to
download your FREE Report

First name

Email

Yes, Send Me My Free Report

Yes, Send Me My Free Report

100% Privacy. I will never spam you!

Resist the temptation to use the latest web graphic effects merely because everyone else seems to be doing it. At all times, simpler is better.

The focus of your page needs to be completely on getting visitors to perform the desired action.

Using too much technology will distract them, and then your message may be lost. Consider also the increased loading time of a page that is multimedia heavy.

Never use flash (Flash is a multimedia and software platform used for creating vector graphics, animation, browser games, rich Internet applications, desktop applications, mobile applications and mobile games.)

Visitors do not want to wait for a page to load. Tell them, clearly, in your first paragraph, that they need to enter their information in the box (and tell them where it is)in order to have their permission to send them the requested "item of value".

Step 2:

Make sure your Landing Page is exactly what they are looking for.

Prospects were driven to your Landing Page from many different points of contact. Let them see what they want immediately. Do not make them search your Landing Page for the required information.

We teach you how to make a great Landing Page in less than 10 minutes. Don't mix and match, create a new page for every single offer you promote.

This has a secondary benefit to you in keeping track of which Landing Pages are successful. You also need to make sure that customers arrive at the exact information they expect. That it is why it is important that your promotions lead visitors to relevant landing pages, and not the home page of your website.

With only seconds to keep their attention, you cannot risk losing your customer's focus by forcing them to search for the information they need from your home page.

Step 3:

Keep the design and text simple. (The K.I.S.S. rule applies here).

The key goal here is to minimize any page distractions.

"Plain Vanilla" Landing Pages convert at a rate **31% higher** than ones filled with graphics and extensive copy.

Remember, this is not a sales page, it is a lead capture page.

Work your text into Bold Headlines and Short Bullet Points.

Cut out all the crap about how smart you are, and all the other self-promoting BS. No one cares about you.

If you promised them a free lesson on how to get their mute parrot to talk, then just have them opt-in and give them their free lesson. Your first goal is accomplished when they take that action. Make damn well sure that what you send to them cures their problem.

Step 4:

Use photos sparingly.

Photos and images are good to use on Landing Pages to give the proper visual representation.

However, only use 1 photo.

Use a picture of a Parrot on your Landing Page, it would be small, and somewhere in the upper left side of page, so it does not interfere with the opt-in box on the right side of the page. The picture is there so that a visitor gets an immediate visual connection and reassures them that they have arrived at the right place.

Keep the picture simple and clean, without an excessive amount of color. Make sure it is a sharp image. Any image out of focus shows as a poorly crafted page.

Step 5:

Bring Brand value to your page.

At the bottom of your Landing Page, you want to use connective images as liberal as possible.

Use badges and logos, such as your social connection buttons, Better Business Bureau, safe shopper logos, privacy protection logos, etc. etc.

Use membership buttons like belonging to the "National Parrot Rescue Club".

The bottom of the page is to give your prospective client a comfort zone. They want to feel a connection to the offering you have, and they do that when they feel comfortable.

This step is known as **transference of goodwill.** Brand yourself as someone that can be trusted.

Now that you have the 5 elements that make a great Landing Page, you can work through the process of "why" you are making this Landing Page.

We always make and design our Landing Pages as if someone was paying us to do it for them.

When we use this mindset, we know we always want to impress the person who has hired us. Therefore, we create the best possible Landing Page without question.

The Cornerstones of your Landing Pages

(What-How-Easy)

1. A landing page should clearly articulate what the consumer is going to get.
2. A landing page should make it clear how the consumer is going to get it.
3. A landing page should make it easy for the consumer to get what they want.

This is the thought that you want running through the heads of your prospective clients when they first see your Landing Page: **What, How and Easy**.

When you give them that experience, more than half your challenge has been accomplished.

Note: The idea that more choices make people happier has been proven to be a psychological fallacy time and again.

This **"paradox of choice"** reveals that when given multiple options, the decision ends up being not to make any decision at all.

An effective landing page asks for one specific action, and that's it.

Focus on to actually clearly ask for that one specific action, it will be a big conversion killer if you don't.

Look at the example below, it projects a clean image, gives the benefits in a bullet point presentation, it asks for the name and email, shows a small picture of the free book.

The theme of the Landing Page is done in one color, (keeping green in the eye of the prospective client).

It then tells them exactly what they will receive, and, as an added inducement, it throws in a $5.00 discount coupon. (Note that they didn't say 10% or 20% off). They gave a clear and defined benefit for the reader to opt-in.

Note: We do not advise asking the last name of the prospect.

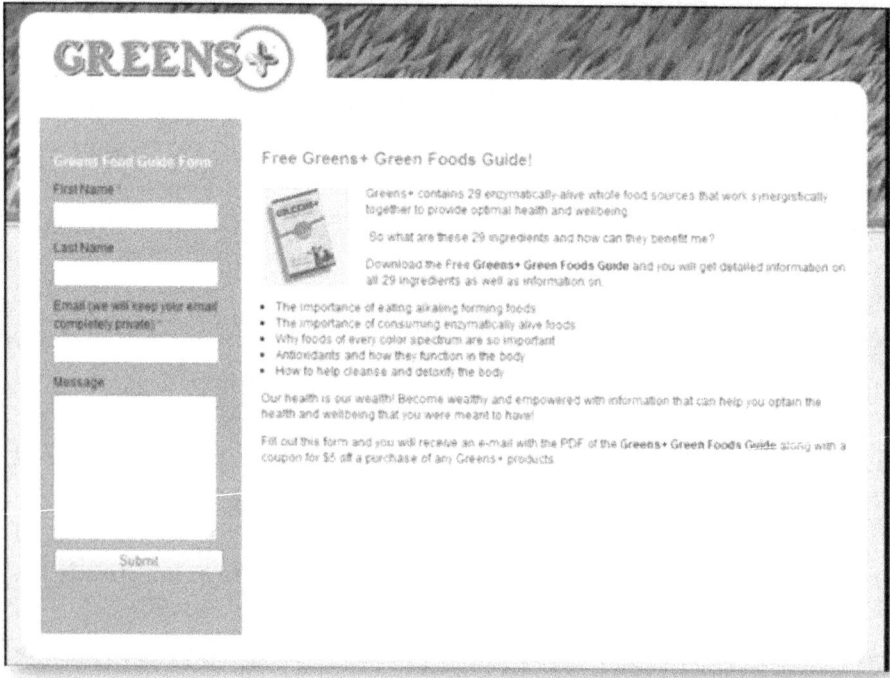

This is clearly a well thought out and presented Landing Page. This is also a great page for testing purposes. We would recommend that this should have the opt-in box on the right side of the page, instead of the left side.

We also would hesitate to include the message box, and reserve that for the actual sales/order page. Instead of using the word "submit", something like "get your copy now" or "where do we send your book" or something to that effect would be preferred.

Now even though this is a well thought out Landing Page, they have made one grievous error.

They used the word "free" as their leading word.

This word, as you know from our list of words to avoid, is a Google spam killer word. The way the sentence is crafted in the headline may lead people to believe that they are getting "free" greens. This occurred because the name of their company is Greens+. In reality, they are giving away a Green Foods Guide. Which to this particular market niche is a valuable product.
The headline should have been:

Green Foods Guide-compliments of Greens+ (their logo)

This would have encompassed their keywords plus their URL and not have any words that would raise a red flag with the search engine spiders.

At this point in your learning curve, we would like you to do some homework by clicking on some of the links you will find on Twitter that are designed to bring you to a specific Landing Page. Analyze and critique the pages you come across.

Certainly if you find some good ones, you want to make a copy and use them to craft your own page(s). There are good and bad elements in all Landing Pages.

Disregard the bad and incorporate the good into your own work. This will save you many hours in your own design work.

Well folks, you have some work to do, and we are burning daylight here.

Over the next 2 boxes, we will be giving you instructions on how to effectively use your Landing Pages in all of your campaigns.

See you all on the other side of Box30.

BOX 30

"Tinker to Evers to Chance"

Landing Page Doorway to your Sales Funnel

The legendary Chicago Cubs trio at the beginning of the 20th century became synonymous with perfection at the double play. In the same manner, develop your sales funnel campaign, in the same way the ballplayers did: have a clear system already set up.

This is the mantra used when crafting the guideline for the instruction in Box 29: "what-how-easy".

When we think of this mantra, it keeps us focused on the steps we wish to accomplish in putting together our marketing campaigns.

Now, you should have completed the assignment in Box 29 and gathered information from exploring links to Landing Pages on various social sites.

You should have a clear understanding of the format that you wish to use. The construction of your Landing Page should now begin.

Once this is completed, you will no longer have to devote time to it, and you will be ready to start earning from your efforts.

With that thought in mind, we have laid out 10 tips to make sure you construct your Landing Page properly, and it delivers the results you want.

Ten Landing Page Funnel Optimization Tips.

Title Tag - Your title tag of your marketing funnel should include the keyword phrases you are searching for. Most sites will use the pipe character "|" as a divider to include some keywords twice. The greatest number of characters should not exceed 70.

Meta Description - The meta description of your marketing sales funnels is found by search engines and then analyzed to see your website relevance to the search term entered. The length of the meta description is kept under 160 characters.

H1 and H2 tags - The Term H tag simply means header tag. Also include your keyword in both heading tags on the homepage of your marketing sales funnel. A H3 tag is an option that can also be added with your keyword to the page.

Images - When using images on your marketing funnel homepage make sure that before you insert or upload an image that it is renamed with your keyword e.g."keyword.jpg". When uploaded to the home page of your marketing sales funnel the alt attribute description is added to the image using the keyword to describe the image in text format. or the image will be ignored by the spiders.

Web Analytics - Install Google web analytic to check the progress of search engine traffic and other web traffic coming to your marketing sales funnel site.

Site-map - A XML Site-map on your site allows the search engines to discover the important elements on your page which otherwise could be missed by the search engine crawlers. The XML Site-map page will list all the components on the page.

Inbound links - Other sites will link to your marketing sales funnel and create inbound links, which gives more authority to that page in the eyes of the search engines. This will make your site more competitive for keywords that you are competing for with other similar sites. This process is simply known as back linking. Therefore, when a site links to different pages on your site that are then linked indirectly to another page this process is then known as deep linking.

Page Index-able - This term is an important phrase to understand as when your marketing sales funnel page is index-able it means that it will appear in search engine results. Sometimes you will need to ping your site to alert search engine crawlers to come visit your site. You are letting them know that you have new content posted and you want them to index it which can take between 24/48 hours.

Page Loading Time - Although this does not affect SEO results very much it is still an important factor of the marketing sales funnel as the homepage of your funnel needs to load fast so that visitors stay on your site. Bounce rate statistics are collected after users click on your site and leave immediately before the page has loaded. Your Google analytic will explain this information in greater detail.

Keyword Placement - The keyword placing strategy is far too important not to share with you. When adding text to your marketing funnel homepage include your keyword at the start of the first sentence of the first paragraph and also at the end of the last paragraph. You then must insert your keyword throughout the content keeping a keyword density of about 3% and keeping it looking natural on the homepage of your marketing sales funnel. Now that you understand the mechanics of your Landing Page, let us delve into the process of moving it forward.

Let us recap so you have the ideas fresh in your mind.

1) You have clearly identified the niche market you wish to pursue.
2) The keyword research for this niche has been completed and you clearly know what this market has been searching for.
3) You have purchased the URL(s) that targets the words used by the niche market to find you. Get the highest search term you can as your URL. In a future box we have a complete tutorial on the construction of URL's.
4) Your new website or blog has been constructed and filled with the content that is of the most interest to your niche.
5) You have selected the end product you want to sell to your target market, or you have the affiliate product you have targeted to promote.
6) You have set up your own "Tinker to Evans to Chance" process:
7) Social Media should be directing targets to:
   a. your Landing Page Links
   b. your Content Pages
   c. your Sales Page

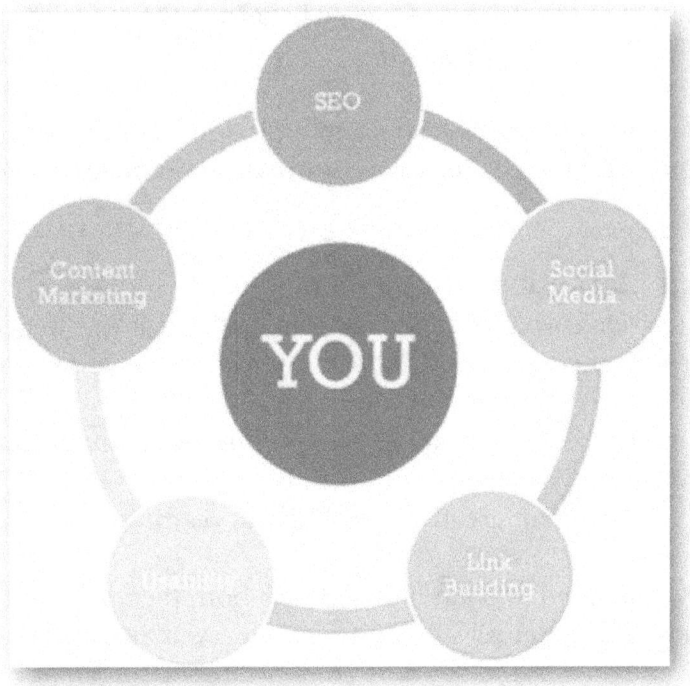

Please notice that it is **"YOU"** that is the center of all campaigns. The logo in the bottom left of this diagram **"Usability"** will be the focus of your Landing Page development.

Make it "easy for your target market"

It cannot be stress enough. Usability & Information Architecture SEO's should value the importance of good site usability. Site usability refers to how your objects are placed on your page and if the information you provide on your site is useful for the users, and easy to use and navigate.

Learning about information architecture is critical as well since it's all about how you organize content on your site, decide on your folder structure, and how you label elements on your site.

This is often an area where SEO's make mistakes especially when they take a keyword approach to IA.

Again, as competition increases and attention span of users decreases, it's important to not let your visitors drop off your site.

Content Marketing

Content is really what engages users and is a great way to get visitors into your marketing funnel. So it's essential as an SEO (Somebody who uses Search Engine Optimization techniques) you possess this skill. Content marketing can be divided into two main tasks:

Content creation and Content distribution.

As a SEO you need to be well versed with both pieces of content marketing strategy, especially content creation. As a SEO, it's your job to act as a gatekeeper and support content ideas that can add value to search engines and users. Basic skills like keyword research, finding content gaps, and distributing your content will come in handy. We have all the outlines for this process in a future box. However, we are not delving into the area of content creation at this point, since we have 2 boxes that cover this area, with all the tools you will need to be able to do it like an expert.

We will instruct you how to use Google Reader in conjunction with Google Alerts to create your very own powerful content monitoring system. Monitoring your niche is extremely important because it allows you to react quickly to realign your Landing Page and engage your affiliate marketing almost instantly.

Right now, let's concentrate on building and optimizing your Landing Page, and creating the best URL for it, so that you can start earning from it.

In Box 31 we will do an actual affiliate product launch, so you can monitor your own commissions and test the effects of various landing pages on your profits.

Folks, we have work to do. We are burning daylight here, so we will see you all on the other side of Box 31.

Rich & Marty

BOX 31

FINDING THE "SWEET SPOT"

Think of the numbers 200 million and 6 thousand

In Box 31, you will learn the significance of the 2 numbers listed above.

Each one of these numbers will be very valuable in your affiliate marketing, direct marketing and content marketing campaigns.

For many of you, the number 200 million will be a total game changer. For many of you, the number 6 thousand will create multiple niches that you have not thought of prior.

Each of these numbers will have a totally different meaning and a totally different end result for all of you. And you will be guided step by step, for whichever number you decide to direct your business towards.

First, there are two key concepts that you must understand. You will understand what will happen in the future, and, no, we do not have a crystal ball.

We have is a keen perception of what the internet "major markets" are going to do in the next 2 to 3 year, and have been closely observing the trends of the two "giants" of the internet, Google and Amazon.

We have watched their "beta" testing programs on the deep web for many months now, and know that they are successful with them. It makes pure economic sense for them to continue with them.

First, we will discuss Amazon. From its inception Amazon has set its goals to become among the world's largest retailer. Of course, we all know they have succeeded.

However, it has also achieved a status that few people realize. Amazon has also become one of the world's largest search engines. You see, Amazon's core structure is pure search engine.

Search any product in the world and Amazon will be right near the top of any search you can ever think of.

We have learned how to capitalize on this amazing search engine by partnering with Amazon Stores, and we have also learned how to propel your product and service to the top of the Amazon rankings. This will be covered in great detail a little later.

Right now our purpose is to get you thinking about Amazon as a search engine, not just a shopping portal. When you grasp this concept, you will be more knowledgeable that 99% of the on-line marketers today. Therefore, you'll be in position to reap great rewards from this.

Now to Google.

Amazon has evolved from one of the largest retailer in the world, to the largest search engine for products and services in the world, and collecting a percentage of all sales made through its searches. Google is now on course to become the largest Affiliate Marketer in the world, and yes, they will succeed.

Google originally positioned itself as a unbiased search engine; it became the 800 pound gorilla in the room.

They derived their revenue from advertising, AdWords, AdSense, and a host of services in the search and SEO areas.

However, as government regulations, that are really just starting, have curtailed some of the width and breath of these features, Google has started to reorganize and shift from a "ad" platform to an affiliate platform.

This was evident when Google rolled out their "partner straight commission program". Now, at first glance, when you look at this program, you think "Google has finally lost its mind". This is because the "suggested" commission they ask you to bid for is always the asking price of the product you are selling.

Most internet marketers ran away so fast that you could see the smoke trail across the internet, and the comments in the IM chat rooms were, let's say, less than complimentary to Google.

However, if you bear with us for a moment, you will see the brilliance in the approach that Google has taken. Also, you will understand how brilliant you will be to take advantage of it.

Going forward, it will take 2 to 3 years before some of the IM people realize what a great deal this is, and, lucky for us, most of them will never get it. In any event you will be so far ahead of the IM crowd that they will never be able to catch up to you in your niche.

Here is how it works: Assume that you have a e-book you are selling about "Parrot Training".

You have set your price at $9.95. You have signed up to advertise your book on Google's "straight commission platform".

Google now "suggests" to you that the commission you pay them is $9.95 for each sale. This is exactly like the Google CPC campaigns where they "suggest" you pay $0.30 or $0.40 or $1.00 or $5.00 per click, depending on the competition of the keywords you are trying to rank for.

The only difference is that on a CPC campaign, your ad placement is based on the amount you bid.

If Google "suggests" that you bid $1.00, but you decide to bid $0.60 instead, depending on your competition, your Google ranking will be a lot lower, and your ads will not appear in the top tier sites like someone that pays the "suggested" $1.00 CPC that Google suggests.

Wait one dog gone second you say!!!! The "only difference" I mentioned, is that there is no profit on the sale. What have I done, lost my mind.!!!! Well, maybe.

First, let's look back inside the box. You have created a e-book product about your niche. You are the authority on this subject. You have filled it with powerful content that is both relevant and important to your niche.

Your cost is your time and labor.

Plus, a hundred or two on some graphic design and some editing and proofreading.

After this, there is no cost for you to produce your product, because it is a download PDF book that a customer gets from your link once the sale is completed. You sell it for $9.95 and pay Google a commission of $9.95.

So, what do you get?

You get the most powerful search engine in the world working for you.

You get the most powerful affiliate marketer in the world working for you.

You get the finest advertising team in the world working for you.

You get top of page 1 placement on Google for your ads.

You get your ads on hundreds of websites relevant to your niche.

You get the most important commodity in our business handed to you:

The Customer.

All of this cost you some time and some work. Other than that, it cost you zero, nada, zippo.

Handed to you on a silver platter you now have the **"Back End"**.

This is List Building on Steroids.

Which Google gets no future commissions from you.

It's 100% yours.

You have a client list to bring into your sales funnel.

Because the person who bought a e-book on Parrot Training, will also buy from you Parrots, Parrot Vitamins, Parrot Training Videos, Parrot Cages, Parrot Costumes, Parrot Food, Parrot Toys and any other product in the world that pertains to Parrots.

So, when you consider the hundreds of dollars that each person will spend, on products you will offer them, the $9.95 you gave up on the front end to acquire the customer means nothing.

Once you have this client list, a cleverly crafted email marketing campaign will keep them bouncing from:

1) your website
2) your blog
3) your Amazon Partner Store.

You will create a point of purchase in all 3 places. This part of our strategy also avoids the "single point of failure" that plagues many internet marketers.

Ladies and Gentlemen, you have just discovered one **"Sweet Spot"**.

It's only "one" sweet spot because we have several more to share with you. Before we do that, let's make sure you are preparing your campaign for success.

Here's an excerpt from Michael Gerber's book **"The E-Myth Revisited":(We highly recommend you read this book).**

When you set up a model that is the prototype, there are rules you must follow:

The model will provide consistent value to your customers, employees, suppliers, and lenders, beyond what they expect.

The model will be operated by people with the lowest possible level of skill.

The model will stand out as a place of impeccable order.

All work in the model will be documented in Operations Manuals.

The model will provide a uniformly predictable exceptional service to the customer.

The model will utilize a uniform color, dress, and facilities code.

If you are going to create a business that serves your life, you must create an organization that will stand on its own.

You need a model that is systematized so that it functions the same way every time, and can be run by people with the lowest skill level. Then, you can step away. And that is the mark of a true business owner—the ability to enjoy the freedom of owning a business, without the requirement of doing work in the business every day.

OK, now you say, "how do I get started".

The answer has been stated many times in the previous 30 boxes: Find your area of interest, something you are passionate about. This is the area that it will not take you long to become the "go to" expert.

Example from Rich:

About 5 years ago, I met a used car dealer from Cleveland, Ohio. We met at a convention of car dealers in Las Vegas. We both had the same passion for poker, and it turned out we spent many hours playing together, and became good poker buddies.

She was a very intelligent and astute business person.

Over the next 2 years, I was teaching her about building her pre-owned car business on-line.

I realized after several months, that she just did not have the passion for this business. I believe that the fact the business was handed down from her father, left her with little sense of accomplishment.

However, she did have a big passion for on-line marketing. After a short time, I discovered that her real area of interest was the S & M lifestyle she was engaged in with her partner. She explained to me, that there was very little credible information on the internet, and no real sources of quality products.

That is when I suggested to her that she start her own on-line business based on her lifestyle, and provide the members of her niche with the quality information and products that they seek to purchase.

I taught her how to create a wordpress.org blog. The.org blog is necessary in this case, because a .com blog does not allow you full control over the content of your blog.

When you create a .com blog, you sign an agreement that allows WordPress to delete your blog if they find it offensive or objectionable. You could spend a year building a .com blog and then have WordPress shut it down with the flip of a switch. Not exactly an idea of building a sustainable business.

Then, she was taught how to create and build a Forum (you will also learn this in a future box).

We had a custom blog theme built for her, at a cost of approx. $300. Over the next 6 months, 20 different Landing Pages were constructed. So, now she had, a blog, a forum, 20 Landing Pages and a very basic flash website.

Then she followed the blueprint you see below, because Rich found out in his research, that this particular niche, was overwhelming visual. So, most of the interest would be derived from embedded video in the blog, rather than the written content common to most websites.

All her revenue is derived from ads on her Blog and Forum, which the Landing Pages point everyone to. She started out by posting this tweet on the Twitter platform, "I just read this great article on why women love the S&M lifestyle" (a bit.ly link was added to bring interested people to the article.

She was off and running with 900 hits on her article in the first week.

Well, you ask, how did this approach work out for her?

Her 2013 sales of a little over 1.3 million dollars, at about a 63% profit margin rate.

In addition, she has collected almost an equal amount from her affiliates. (You will also learn how to set up a successful affiliate program in a future box).

Now you can't even count how many sub-niches she discovered from her primary niche.

You now have food for thought, and we are burning daylight here. So, let's stop getting ready to get ready, and start setting up your blog ideas.

We will see you all on the other side of Box 32. There you will also find the answer to 200 million and 6 thousand.

Rich & Marty

BOX 32

MARKETING TO EVERYONE IS MARKETING TO NO ONE

As we enter the final phase prior to launching your first successful affiliate marketing campaign, use the headline above as your mantra. "FOCUS" can't be overemphasized It is the most important factor that will lead you to your goals. Remember in the early 2000's when tech-based companies were going public with nothing more than a bright idea?

Investors made a lot of money quick but eventually their gains vanished in a New York minute. The same can happen when you place your entire business in the hands of one merchant or just one campaign or one source of traffic. "Instant success isn't always what it seems to be".

Time, patience, and not giving up are some of the key factors to seeing your long term project through, and you being both a short term AND long term success story! Where are you with your business? Let's get started and give it some legs.

Making Money on Pinterest.

Pinterest not only allows, but also encourages e-commerce on their site, and that is rare among social media platforms. They make it easy for you, the seller, to market a product. And they also make it easy for users to find products they might be interested in purchasing. Example from Rich:

> *I had my admin assistant research all the books on Amazon dealing with Parrot Training. My assistant features those books via my Amazon affiliate link. We use those Amazon features on Pinterest, and because I've asked my assistant to add the price of each book, all my additions are now part of the Pinterest Gifts page—and they are categorized by price.*
>
> *This is a brilliant way for affiliate marketers and entrepreneurs to take advantage of Pinterest's commerce-friendly features.*
>
> *I know it might sound complicated, but I can assure you that adding affiliate products to Pinterest is super-easy. I've removed all the guesswork for you by detailing step-by-step how you can add your own affiliate products to Pinterest to boost your affiliate commissions.*
>
> *Before I get started, I want to show you where all the Gifts are featured on Pinterest, because this will give you a good idea of the power of this feature. When you sign into your account, you'll want to click on the Pinterest logo to land on your homepage, featuring the latest pins from people you follow.*

On your homepage, you'll notice a Gift tab at the top of the Pinterest site: When you click on the drop-down button, you can select gifts by price range, or you can click and select to view all the latest products for sale added by users:

You will notice that all products have price tags. This means users know the price of a product before clicking on the photo to find out more.

How to add your first money making affiliate product to Pinterest?

1) Categorize your affiliate products by creating separate boards Right now, I have one board for my Amazon books and another board for products related to video marketing and I intend on adding more boards as I add more affiliate products.

2) Add a new board:

3) To add a new board, you'll first need to click on the Add button at the top of your homepage.

4) Select create a board.

5) Name your board. Make sure the name is search engine friendly. It might be tempting to use a "creative" name, but remember that Pinterest is a search engine, and optimized boards will show up on Google search results. (This is why followers of "Internet Marketing Defined" will be so far ahead of the crowd, and the affiliate marketing curve, because we realize that Pinterest is a SEARCH ENGINE, disguised as a social media network).

6) I've selected to name my board "Books for Training Parrots". (KISS) How to optimize Pinterest to get more traffic and clicks to your affiliate product:

7) Add your URL Don't forgot to always add your URL to everything you pin on Pinterest so people can find your Landing Page.

8) Since each additional pin contains my affiliate links, I've added the URL to one of my main sites in the description box. Upload your affiliate product to a Pinterest board

9) Upload a pin instead of adding a pin (because you need to include your affiliate link), you'll need to upload a pin—that is a photo—from your computer:

10) Select the right board

11) You now need to select the appropriate board ... in other words, the board you just created for all these affiliate products. So I'll select the "Books for Training Parrots" board:

12) Add a description and URL

13) You now need to add a description and add the URL to where you want people to land or your affiliate link. Although you're allowed 500 words, keep the description short and sweet because you want to make sure your affiliate link or the link to your main site shows up.

14) Point people to your Landing Page via a URL and hide your affiliate link behind the image in order to add your affiliate link behind the image, you'll need to go back and edit the pin you just uploaded.

15) You can add your affiliate link inside the description box, but if you do, you'll want to make sure it's "cloaked" (aka masked) or you'll want to use the services of a link shortened like bit.ly.

16) If you add a long "affiliate" URL that screams "affiliate link!" it's unlikely anyone will click on it.

17) Edit your pin in order to add an affiliate link behind the image—and one that will be accessible every time someone clicks on the image you just uploaded you will need to edit the pin.

18) Once you click on the red Pin It button, you'll be redirected to a page where you can edit the pin: How to add your affiliate link to Pinterest

19) Add your link (this part is easy): you will simply need to add your affiliate link inside the Link box. This will allow the image you uploaded to be fully click-able, and it'll automatically redirect Pinterest users to any product or service you're promoting via your affiliate link.

20) Add your product to GIFTS. In order to get you product added to the Gifts page, and to get those cool little price tags featured on your pin, you simply need to add the price to the description box.

21) The price appears the second Pinterest's search engine recognizes you've added a price and the dollar sign ($), it will automatically add the cool price in the upper left corner of your image.

22) Within a few seconds, your new pin, containing your affiliate link, will be featured on the homepage of every one of your followers.

It's hard to tell how long it will take for pins with price tags to appear under the Gifts category, because there are so many new additions going up all the time. That being said, your pin is automatically added to the homepage of your followers!

This is why it is important to build out your following on Pinterest. However, since you are building your follower base on the criteria that you all have the same general interests; you have a very targeted audience, that will be highly responsive.

There are quite a few little steps to adding affiliate products to our Pinterest profile, but as you can see, it's quite easy.

In example above, the Amazon product and the Amazon affiliate link were used, but you can use the same logic for pretty much any product.

The advantage with Amazon is that you could actually include the affiliate link as it appears in the description box without putting off viewers, because everyone has come to associate Amazon with quality!

If you haven't yet explored adding affiliate products to Pinterest, it's a great way for marketers to increase sales of affiliate products, and it's also a great way to increase the visibility of your Landing Page and main website among Pinterest users. The beauty of this whole process is that you can add UNLIMITED boards and UNLIMITED affiliate products to create multiple income streams.

Now, as stated in many previous boxes, the affiliate marketing process is to generate income that is necessary to purchase the tools you will need to further enhance your business. Nothing is sweeter than to use OPM (other people's money) to build your empire.

One of these tools you can use (see the link below) costs around $50.00, and it is used to build your one-page website Landing Pages. Explore the free features of this tool and play around with it to get familiar before you purchase it. Make it a goal to purchase it with the affiliate commissions that you generate through Pinterest. Instapage.com

Well folks, you now have a little work to do in setting up your product lines on Pinterest.

Since we are burning daylight here, it's time for you get started and get some income streams working for you.

Rich & Marty

BOX 33

THE VALUE SWAP

A s we have mentioned in previous boxes, you need to give something of important value to your prospective customer in order to get something of value: their point of contact. It's important to think seriously about the "value" you will be giving. It needs to be relevant to your prospects needs, and it must be something that will make their life easier, more rewarding, or simplified.

So, don't just send or offer to send fluff. If you do, you will not reach your goal.

Why is this Box33 named the way it is?

We didn't just wake up one morning and say "gee, That's a cute name". No, we want you to start thinking about your process as a "campaign". All the elements are planned well in advance of putting your offer into your opt-in box on your Landing page.

You must develop 8 email relationship letters, and they must be in place, and scheduled for broadcast, before you let anyone opt-in to your offer(s).

You need to test the entire sequence on yourself and your master-mind group before it goes live on the internet. (**This step is of the utmost importance**).

Note: In Boxes 30 & 31, we gave you "The 7 Tips for Landing Page Greatness" (In addition a list of 500 words called "The Ultimate List of E-Mail Spam Trigger Words" is available on www.internetvisions-defined.com. Make sure you review this tutorial after you have done your copywriting of the emails that you will use in your sequences.

In order to get you started, we have compiled the "102 Proven Headline Formulas" list. These headlines can be used in your subject line or as the header of your body copy, and you can mix and match these headlines to suit your prospective clients interest.

You can also incorporate 8 of these headlines as your theme in all of your follow up sequences. Whichever "Formula" works best for you, keep in mind that it needs to be consistent with the conversation you will be having through your email sequence:

102 Proven Headline Formulas

Take these fill-in-the blanks templates and complete them to create your own compelling, click-getting headlines.

Get What You Want (Health, Wealth, Relationships, Time and Lifestyle)

1. 10 Money/Time Saving Tips for _____
2. The Secret of Getting the Best Price for Your _____
3. How to Find the Best _____ Deals on the Web
4. Top Gadgets for _____
5. Are _____ Worth the Money?
6. Everything You Need to Know About Getting Cheaper _____
7. Top 10 Tips for Hassle Free _____
8. Best ____ For Under [Price]
9. Unusual but Achievable ____
10. 5 Ways to Boost Your ____ Without Spending More _____
11. Ways to ____ on a Budget
12. 5 Ways to _____ and Profit!
13. 21 Audacious and Creative _____ Ideas
14. Who Else Wants to ____?
15. Now You Can ____ for Free!
16. How to Get _____ in Half the Time
17. 10 Stars and their ____
18. _____ Lifestyles of the Rich and Famous
19. How to Look and Act _____
20. Now You Can Have Get More and Better ____ With Less Effort
21. _____ like a Movie Star
22. 9 Ways You Can ____ Better Than You Deserve
23. How to ____ in 10 Seconds
24. Have a ____ You Can Be Proud Of
25. 21 _____ Conversation Tips
26. Finding Your Perfect _____
27. Plan a Perfect _____
28. What ____ Really Want
29. 7 Signs You Are/Can _____
30. Get ____ Now

Crystal Ball and History

31. The History of _____
32. How _____ Will Impact _____ in [Year]
33. _____ Then and Now
34. 40 Predictions on the Future of ____
35. The Modern Rules of _____
36. ___ Lessons from History
37. The _____Story

Problems and Fears

38. Are _____ a Dying Breed?
39. How to Beat the Fear of _____
40. 10 ____ Scams and How to Avoid Them
41. How Secure Are Your _____?
42. 7 Most Frightening ____
43. Top 10 Scary _____ Facts
44. Outrageous _____ and How They Could Impact You
45. Get Rid of Your _____ Once and For All
46. Could Your _____ be a _____?
47. What Your ____ is Not Telling You About _____
48. Beware _____ and How to Spot them
49. 10 Good Ways NOT to _____
50. How to Safely _____
51. The Unseen/Biggest Dangers of _____
52. _____ Do's and Don'ts
53. 21 Ways to Screw Up _____
54. 10 Reasons Not to _____
55. 7 _____ Danger Signs
56. 7 things _____ Should Never Do

Fact, Fiction, Secrets, Truth and Lies

57. What Everyone Ought to Know about _____
58. ____ Personality Test: What Your ____ Says About You
59. _____ Lies and How to Spot them
60. _____ Facts and Myths
61. The Real Truth About _____
62. 7 Secrets the _____ Experts Don't Want You to Know
63. 101 Most Popular _____ Myths
64. 4 _____ Facts You Need to Know
65. The Secret of Successful _____
66. Little Known Ways to _____
67. Truth and Lies in _____
68. All You Need to Know about _____
69. 10 Lies We Tell Our _____
70. 101 things Not to tell _____
71. Revealed: Why _____
72. How to Spot a Fake _____

How-To Tricks of the Trade

73. When is it Smarter to ____ or ____?
74. Little Known Ways to _____
75. 10 Reasons it's Better to _____
76. How to Plan the Ultimate _____
77. How to _____ Like a _____
78. ____ Jobs You Can Do Yourself
79. Here is a Method That is Helping _____ to _____
80. Here's a Quick Way to _____
81. 7 Creative Ways to _____
82. How to be a _____

83. 9 Surprising Things You Can _____
84. _____ Like an Expert in 10 Easy Steps
85. 21 Expert ____ Tips
86. 5 Reasons You Should _____

Best and Worst

87. Top 10 World's Cheapest/Best/Most Expensive _____
88. The World's Best _____ You Can Actually Afford to Buy
89. The World's Worst Ever _____
90. The World's Most Unusual _____
91. Funniest _____ Stories
92. Sexiest _____ in the World
93. The Top 10 Best and Worst _____ in the World
94. Top 19 Most ____ Friendly ____
95. 100 Useful or Beautiful ____
96. 5 Reasons _____ is Better than _____
97. The World's Top 10 Most Important _____
98. Top 20 Clips About _____ in Films and Television
99. 10 ____ We Don't Want to See ____
100. 21 Most Hilarious _____
101. The World's Worst _____ Advice
102. 10 Reasons ____ is the Worst _____

Presented as: "MyTwentyGroup" Special Report.

The above Headline Formula's will get you started on your thought processes as it pertains to your particular product/information niche.

Box 34 will be a step by step guide to the timing of your email broadcasts for maximum results and the proper alignment of your emails. Also in Box 34 we will guide you through adding video to your email campaign, which we suggest being placed in your second email of the series.

Although the initial set up of your campaign is time intensive, you have to remember that once it is all set, your auto responders will take over and have your campaign running until you decide to hit the "off" switch.

This means that from your initial campaign, you will be earning money for months and even years into the future, all without ever having to visit the campaign again.

That allows you to "Rinse and Repeat" on all your subsequent email campaigns.

Well folks, you have a lot of work to do here in Box33, and we are burning daylight. So let's "stop getting ready to get ready" and put in some of the good old burning the midnight oil.

With that said, we will see you on the other side of Box 34.

Rich and Marty

BOX 34

"Do It Now, Fix It Later"

ffiliate marketing is not a monumental task if you just follow the simple rule above.

When we first started in on-line business marketing, in 1999, the world was a little bit different. No one was purchasing anything on the internet. People did not trust in the internet because they did not know anything about it, and no one would even dare to enter their credit card numbers into cyberspace.

Just think, only 5 years prior to that (1994), no one was using email. It was a totally new concept.

Then we came across a book named the "Cluetrain Manifesto". This book, we believed was a true glimpse into the future, a vision of things to come. We had no idea at that time that this one book would take us on a wonderful journey of learning that would span the next decade of our lives.

It took us more than six months to truly realize that products and services, could, and would, be sold over the internet. All that we knew at that time is that we wanted to be part of it.

We had no idea of what we wanted to sell on-line, but we learned from this book that the "markets" would tell us what to sell and when to sell it.

We became very comfortable in our "excuse zone".

We found several reasons why this wouldn't work or that wouldn't work, until we discovered that the companies involved in the early internet marketing were growing their businesses using commissioned sales agents, as it was known way back then. Today the term is "Affiliate Marketers".

That is when the light went on. **A true.... "ah-ha" moment.**

You see, it doesn't matter what the product or service really is. The Affiliate Marketer in its purest sense is about promoting the products and services of many different companies.

Affiliate Marketing is about creating your own system of promotion.

With this overpowering concept you can now start on your path to become a Master Affiliate Marketer. Now that we have the concept, let us begin the process system:

We have always advocated that you should begin with the biggest, the brightest, the best.

It doesn't get any bigger, brighter, or better than Amazon.com....Let's do some digging.

First: Histrionics.

You might remember in the very early boxes, one of the "gigs" used to get a little cash flowing was selling coupons on eBay.

It is still one of our delights to this day. Think about the early days in this business when a "$5.00 off " coupon from a national pet store chain was cut out of the newspaper, and put on eBay. Someone actually paid $2.00 for it.

To say the least, it was dumbfounding. Who would have guessed that there was a REAL market in coupons? After putting a $.32 stamp on the envelope, and paying eBay a 10 cents commission, $2.00 was deposited in our PayPal account.

A profit of $1.58 was realized. Even though you are not in this business to make $1.58, or $576.70 for the year, if you sell one coupon a day, think about the process. (Although we never met a five hundred seventy-six dollars and seventy cents deposit that we didn't like).

What's important is that a systemic process was created. In 2009, after teaching the system to our admin, for about one hour's work a day we cleared (net) about $14,000 in coupon sales.

It was a whole lot of fun (and is still ongoing). Just go to eBay, type in "coupons". You will discover a new world and find out for yourself. You will be amazed also.

Now to the Big Leagues

In 1995 a new "kid" came on the block. It was an online bookstore, and its first focus was selling cheaper books to college kids. Then they expanded into music.

With CD's, DVD's, etc. We all know the story of the mighty **Amazon. com**

We also know that if anyone in Borders Books read the Cluetrain Manifesto, they would still be in business today. In any event, in Box 25 you learned how to set up an Amazon store.

We did refrain from explaining exactly what you should do with it once you had it all set up.
After setting up our own Amazon store, the quandary of out what we were going to sell came up. Then we realized that we can sell almost every single item that is offered on Amazon.

We originally chose to stay within my niche and promote Parrot items.

First, we went to Amazon and typed in the search box "parrot food". This search brought up the listings of everyone selling parrot food on Amazon. (1,721 results). That number also told us that this was a strong and money making sub-niche (parrot food).

Starting from the #1 listing and after clicking on the heading, a page opens. About 5 lines down, in BOLD GREEN it says "IN STOCK". and there it will tell you who is selling it. The first listing is from a national brand, and it says "Sold by XXXXX and fulfilled by Amazon". This means that the manufacturer of the product shipped it to Amazon's warehouse, and Amazon, in turn, ships it to the customer.

At this moment, we have no interest in this company.

The #2 listing says "Sold by Amazon and Fulfilled by Amazon" …. BINGO…This is what we are looking for.

After you sign onto your Amazon store, search for a product by typing "parrot food". You will then see the product that is sold and fulfilled by Amazon, and you will see the box that that says "get link". This link will appear below:

http://www.amazon.com/Hartz-Bird-Large-Birds-8-Pound/dp/ B000HHLNB6/ref=sr_1_2? ie=UTF8& qid=1359340048& sr=8-2& keywords=parrot+food

Do you see the numbers on the second line, 1359340048? Well, that's our direct affiliate link.

Now, the next step is to go and get a URL shortener, (bit.ly etc. and you will get something that looks likehttp://amzn.to/1kxSEma) Now you can use this as your link on your blog, or in an article on your website, or when you make a comment on a relevant blog, or on your tweets and Facebook comments, and all the Q&A sites that are all over the web.

You get what we're saying here? Anywhere and everywhere you get the opportunity, you place your bit.ly within the content you are promoting.

This is the age old marketing tactic: "Throw enough stuff at the wall and some of it is bound to stick"

When you place your shortened URL in a relevant place and someone clicks on it, it will go directly to the product site that is **"sold and fulfilled by Amazon".** Then Amazon completes the order and says thank you to you by placing your commission dollars in your account.

Example: (twitter) My 5 yr. old Parrot was sick, then I found this great vitamin and diet food, now he is whistling Dixie. (place your link here).

Let's keep Digging

As mentioned above, there were the sites that sold their own products and shipped to Amazon for the fulfillment process. We were not interested in at that moment.

Well, after getting the URL's from all the parrot products that Amazon sells and fulfills directly, take a look at the big time sellers.

NOTE: Just like a listing on Google, if the product is not in the top 10-15 listings on Amazon, it might as well be arriving at the third traffic light that is not working in Siberia.

Now let's go to these sellers on Amazon, find their website, and see if they have an affiliate program. If they do, sign up, get all the necessary link information, and promote them in the same way.

People will buy from these companies because they are nationally established brands, and, therefore, you don't want to exclude them. (and they always pay a higher commission than Amazon does). So, you can sell less and make more!

If they don't have an affiliate program, so be it. But that is not the end of it all. We found on these sites a GOLDMINE of information that you can copy and paste. Realize that they have articles and blogs, listings of "clubs", lists of veterinarians, and information that would take you days to find and use. What a bonanza!

Either way, you win.

You can achieve total niche domination for a particular product that falls into your niche, by promoting both the Amazon products and the company products that are competing with Amazon for the same product line.

How sweet is this?

Sort of reminds us of how Mobile Oil became a worldwide power-house by selling gas and oil to the USA, Germany and Japan during WWII.

This is why previous Boxes taught to set up multiple accounts in all the social networks that relate to a specific niche. This puts you on the path to become a Master Affiliate Marketer; you will define and redefine your niches, to a point of maximum profitability.

You will get expanded information on this in a future box.

Now folks, we have a little work to do; We are burning daylight here, so "Do It Now, Fix It Later".

See you in Box 35.

Rich & Marty

Illustration

Vision of a New York minute.

and

How it affects your product distribution.

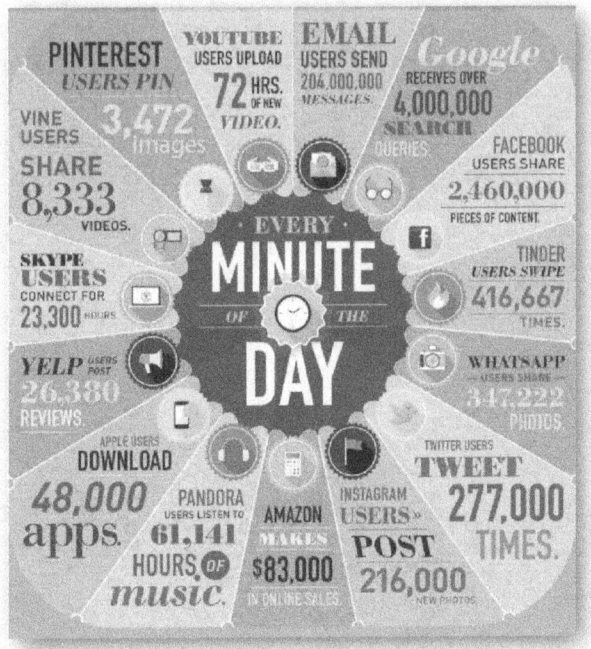

When viewing a chart like the one above, it will make you realize how incomprehensible these numbers are.

Are you competing with all this "white noise" that clutters the internet every single minute?

Just ponder the magnitude of the numbers in the chart. Rich said, "it brings me back to one of my very first business lessons that I learned from joke that I heard decades ago."

Two guys are camping. They hear a hungry, angry bear crashing around outside their tent.

One guy starts putting on his running shoes. The other guy asks, "Why are you putting on your running shoes? You can't outrun a bear."

The first guy says, "I don't have to outrun the bear. I just have to outrun you."

By observing the chart, you have learned the meaning of **"Selling to everyone is selling to no one"**.

BOX 35

STARTING AND MANAGING A CAMPAIGN

Rule # 1   GIVE first.
Rule # 2   Find and Solve their problem.
Rule # 3   Deliver what you promise.
Rule # 4   Take yours on the back end.

I nternet marketing campaigns are extremely powerful, when they are well thought out and planned properly. There are most likely 100 different ways to manage a campaign, and we do not look down on any of them.

What is created here for you is a highly defined **10 Step** program:

Step 1
Website Architecture: This is the most important and critical element in your marketing campaign.

Every piece of content you produce, that is intended to drive traffic to your website, will fail if your site is not properly constructed prior to sending out your first tweet, Facebook notice, Quora inquiry, YouTube publish, etc.

Your site must be structured to accept all communication devices, with mobile-ready being the number one priority. On April 21, 2015, Google officially added "mobile-friendliness" as a worldwide ranking factor.

If you're not providing a mobile-friendly experience for your potential customers, they'll bounce off your website and go to your competitor, whose website is easier to utilize.

Marty Saposnick is, without reservation, the most knowledgeable Digital Architect on the internet today. Marty will evaluate your site, free of charge, for anyone of our readers who need assistance in this area.

Step 2
Review and Analyze all your setup systems:

- **Website**
- **Autoresponder**

- **Google Analytics**
- **Google Authorship**
- **Social Media Bio**
- **Google AdWords**
- **Facebook Business Ads**
- **LinkedIn Ads**
- **Landing pages**
- **Email Marketing**
- **Re-Targeting**

This is now the time to bring your mastermind team into play. Designate who responsible for what part of the campaign they will manage. They will now have to set up the benchmarks necessary to track where your campaign is going.

Example: Social Media Bio: Let us say you are active on 8-10 social media sites, the person who manages this portion must ensure that every single site has the same biographical information and that it all points to one destination: YOUR website. This is important on many different levels. Now that Google indexes something as simple as a Tweet, you better be linked to all your profiles without fail. Everything in the above list **must** connect.

There are several tools on the internet that assist you in doing this, and we have 6 listed on our website with the pros and cons of each one.

Step 3
Give your knowledge for free.
Let's be reasonable here. Potential clients have come to your site because they have a problem to solve. or need an answer to a question. Now if this potential client receives a solution from you, and it was given as a gift, you have gained their trust and respect. The next time they have a related problem, and they will, you will be their first "go to" guy.

Meanwhile, they have given you their email address to receive this free solution, so they now become part of your marketing funnel.

Example: There is a famous chef from New Orleans, who also has a show on TV. Now when you go to his website, "BAM", you are thrilled at the content. He gives you free recipes for as many dishes that you could imagine to cook.

What does he gain from giving away "free recipes"? He is growing a FOLLOWING that allows him to sell the rights to his products including cookware, cookbooks, television shows, and food products in a $50 million agreement with Martha Stewart Living.

Please remember this guy was just a cook. Then he learned "Internet Marketing".

Step 4
Landing Pages.
Make your campaign work for you. Keep it very simple and relevant.

Your landing page(s) need to be designed to accomplish one action. Drive your prospective clients to your site. Do not make it hard for them. Do not make it confusing. Make sure the first thing they see is what you promised to give them.

You should start with six landing pages for each campaign. This will allow you to split test each page in order to see which ones are the most effective. Also, you'll find out which landing page works best on a particular social media site.

At this point your system needs to be correctly set up on your auto responder. When a prospect clicks on a link it not only takes them to your site, but also sends the email address to your auto responder and into your sales funnel. This must be tested and retested to make sure it is working properly.

It is not difficult to set up landing pages; there are several programs, like Unbounce and Instapage that do the job for you at low cost.

Step 5
Email Marketing
This step is integral to your marketing campaign; there is no success without it.
You need to set up your email sequence in advance of offering your first product, it has to consist of seven emails and each has to be crafted to say the same message without being redundant. It will be very rare that a prospective client will purchase anything on their first visit to your site.

Consequently, it is crucial that you work with your autoresponder to see that all the emails are literate and void of grammatical errors. Also, that the sequence is delivered just as you have planned it.

Marty and I use AWeber for our autoresponder. We have found this to be easy to use, and they have really great tutorials. Since this is such an important part of your campaign, it needs to be delegated to the most dependable member of your team.

This leads us to Step 6 and the importance of how you follow up.

Step 6
Educate, do not sell.
No one likes to be sold to. Everyone enjoys making an informed and intelligent decision. So, your email follow up should inform and

educate your prospective client. You need to nurture your list. It is a valuable asset, don't hammer away at a sales pitch. This approach rarely works, and it is annoying to most of the population.

Don't use the old and tired approach of "offer ending soon" or "limited supply" that worked in the 1990's, but **it does not work in today's sophisticated marketplace**.

There are several examples of these follow up email letters on our site; they are free for you to use in any context that you wish. So please stop by and avail yourself to these creative tools.

Step 7
Develop a content marketing calendar.
At the beginning of each campaign take the time to organize calendars for all the individual social media sites. This is not a one size fits all proposition, since diverse prospective clients tend to congregate on specific social media sites. What works well on Facebook, would most certainly fall flat on LinkedIn, and what works on Twitter may not go over well on YouTube.

Using a tool like Hootsuite will certainly speed up this very time consuming task. The true purpose of using a content calendar is to show your audience that you are organized.

You must develop a separate strategy calendar for every social media platform that your audience participates in.

This requires research on your part in order to identify exactly where this audience hangs out.

Step 8
Establish your Goals and Objectives.
A detailed set of marketing objectives is essential to the success of any kind of business. Writing down a list of goals and marketing objectives can lead to larger success in terms of profit and revenues.

In order for marketing objectives to be both valid and efficient, they should be: specific, measurable, achievable, relevant and time sensitive. There is no point of setting objectives if you don't set a time limit for yourself.

There needs to be accountability in goals and objectives. Members of your mastermind team share the responsibility of adhering to the benchmark performance set.

Step 9
SEO
The importance of SEO (Search Engine Optimization) in your campaign is not limited to your website's home page. You can optimize specific pages on your site that you wish to take a visitor directly to.

Search Engine Optimization, or SEO, refers to the art and science behind everything we do to ensure that your site is found by the search engine spiders and ranked highly for maximum visibility.

Search Engine Result Pages (SERPs) are what you see when you enter a query into a search engine like Google, Bing or Yahoo. The SERP listings are called "organic" search results, because they happen naturally – you did not pay to advertise the results.

You can optimize your landing pages and posts and tweets when you include your top keywords.

The necessity of SEO is paramount, and a recent Facebook milestone teaches us the importance of it.

On Monday August 24, 2015, Facebook logged 1 Billion visitors in one single day. Also, 83% of those visitors were from outside the United States.

On our website we have a free tutorial on how to optimize your site to reach audiences in many different countries and specific cities within those countries. This is a goldmine and it is overlooked by 99.9% of marketers today.

Step 10
Promote Aggressively and Relentlessly
Now that you have the campaign elements, it is time to take action. When you have completed all your system setups and have tested and retested them to perfection, it is now time to get your message out there.

Do your market research correctly and you will be selling what the consumer wants to buy, and not what you happen to be selling at the moment.

If this confuses you, then go back to the top of this box and look at rule # 2.

Rich & Marty

BOX 36

My Personal Pyramid

Y ou've learned many things in the previous Boxes and you will be learning many more concepts in future Boxes.

At this time in your development you should start developing your path to Internet Marketing success!

It is time to start your 4-part process, each independent of one another, and yet, all are connected at every level.

On the pyramid chart below you can see the natural flow of a successful internet marketing business. At the base of the pyramid note the 2 most important steps:

First is the NEED to create your plan, just get a notepad and a pen and start writing it. It does not have to have a structure;

this is not a business plan you are going to present to a bank or a group of investors.

It is your personal plan, and it must have a goal. Let's just say for now that you want to create a business that will make you a set amount of money in the next 2 or 3-year period. Write it down, the exact amount you wish to own.

(If you have trouble doing something like this, I strongly suggest you go to Amazon and buy Goals: Setting and Achieving Them on Schedule by Zig Ziegler) **Buy the DVD**, not the book. The visual impact of this great man, one of our mentors, will leave a lifelong lasting impression on you.

The next, and most important step up the pyramid is "Discipline and Focus".

You have already heard me say "Focus" about a hundred times in previous Boxes and you will hear it more from me in future Boxes, I also give you a tutorial on How, Where and Why to focus in a future Box.

You have already heard us say "Focus" about a hundred times in previous Boxes and you will hear it more in future Boxes. You will also get a tutorial on How, Where and Why to focus in a future Box.

The IM Success Map

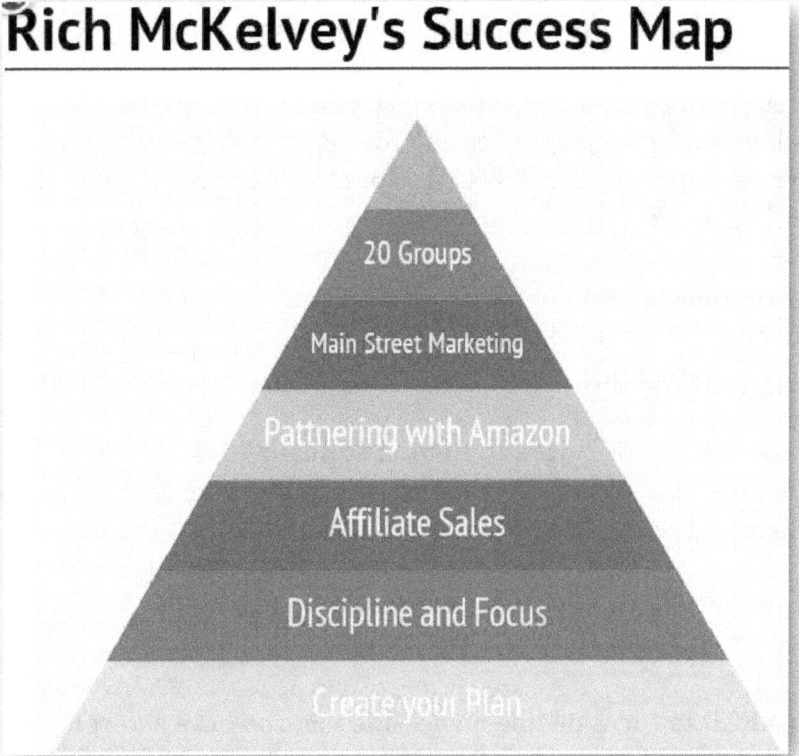

Rich McKelvey's Success Map

- 20 Groups
- Main Street Marketing
- Pattnering with Amazon
- Affiliate Sales
- Discipline and Focus
- Create your Plan

Let us start with the 3rd. Step of the pyramid, which is the actual beginning of the money making process.

Take one moment to reflect on the words to the song "The Rose" by Bette Midler.

> When the night has been too lonely
> And the road has been too long,
> And you think that success is only
> For the lucky and the strong,
> Just remember in the winter

> Far beneath the bitter snows
> Lies the **seed** that with the sun's love
> In the spring becomes the rose.

As you focus on that particular verse from her song, you will see that Affiliate Marketing is the "Seed" for your business. It allows you to move forward and get the seed capital you will need to implement your business goals.

Face it, you are going to have to make some investments in your business, and the smart way is to earn it through a little sweat equity in Affiliate Marketing.

Nowhere is it more evident, than in Affiliate Marketing, where discipline and focus pay off; so plan to "seed" away ½ of your profits from affiliate marketing in order to grow your business.

Failure to heed this sage advice will just put you on the treadmill, and you will plug along until you finally give up.

You NEED to focus on one niche (one that you have a working knowledge of) and develop the discipline to work only in that niche until you start to produce results. Everything you do has to be centered on driving members of that niche to your sales funnel.

Do not make the mistake of believing that you will make untold fortunes working in this "seedling" niche. It won't happen. However, you can earn a decent, steady cash flow from your initial niche, thereby providing you with the capital necessary to grow your business.

If, by chance, this Affiliate Marketing appeals to you, and you have decided to make that your primary business, you will learn shortly how to apply the "**rinse and repeat**" formula to this business sector.

OK, so let us begin the affiliate marketing process in the easiest of all venues. We go back to Amazon and start doing our niche searches for products

EXAMPLE:

- Assume you are in the "Pet" niche.
- Do an Amazon Best seller search for pet products.
- You can assume that you'll come up with "Frontline" flea and tick killer.
- It has been the #1 seller in Amazon pet products for 2-3 years.
- It sells for about 60 bucks and you earn a $4.00 to $5.00 commission for selling it.
- The important thing here is that **you are working "with" Amazon and not against them**.
- So, you take this nationally known product and put it in your Amazon store.
- Then, you write a blog post on your "pet" blog, expounding the benefits of keeping the household pets free of ticks and fleas, as well as protecting humans from Lyme disease, etc.
- You put your affiliate link here and there within the blog post, and whenever someone clicks on the link, you will earn 5 bucks from Amazon. Also make sure you are writing a short review of the product and how you use it yourself, etc.etc.

Then, you write a blog post on your "pet" blog, expounding the benefits of keeping the household pets free of ticks and fleas, as well as protecting humans from Lyme disease, etc.

You put your affiliate link here and there within the blog post, and whenever someone clicks on the link, you will earn 5 bucks from Amazon. Also make sure you are writing a short review of the product and how you use it yourself, etc.etc.

Now, since you are establishing yourself as an authority on pets through your blog, you will be able to repeat this process with many pet products, pet health aids, pet comfort products, pet nutrition, the list is endless.

As your "pet' blog grows, advertisers who specialize in pet products, will come to you to place their ads on your blog.

In a future Box you will learn how to accelerate this process through "ad networks".

There is a definite science to getting multiple ad networks to pitch your blog, and we will teach you how to do it.

Once your blog is established, you can now promote hundreds of pet services that have affiliate programs. These programs pay you 50% to 80% of all sales you generate.

For example, through an affiliate program relating to TrainPetDog. com, payout was a whopping 80% on each and every product sold. They have a monthly paid membership program that has over 50,000 active members (and that is just dogs).

Understand that there are no limits on what you can promote and sell through your blogsite. It just has to be real, and you have to give information that has genuine value to readers. You must engage your audience through your comment section, once they see you as a trusted source, they will buy from you.

Soon, they will be buying your private label brand for pet products, you see, every manufacturer of pet products also offers you the option of putting your own label on the product. So you can be developing holistic vitamins for direct sale, and also on Amazon, and of course you will have your own affiliate program so others can make money for themselves and for you.

Are you beginning to understand that all of the 4-part process is independent of each other, yet very tightly connected?

It's time for you to start approaching your entry to the market. It does not matter what your particular niche is. This process can be set for any physical product or digital product or coaching product.

So now you say "I can't do this because I am not a blogger, or I don't have a blog, or I don't even know how to start a blog!

JUST UNDERSTAND

Now that we have the excuses out of the way, it is time for action.

In the next Box we will give you a step by step instruction on how to set up and launch a **PROFESSIONAL** blog in under 2 hours.

So, we are burning daylight here folks. You have a lot of thinking to do on your niche, and we will see you on the other side of Box37.

Rich & Marty

BOX 37

THE BLOG ZONE

"The Center of your Gravity"

First and foremost, before you start to build your blog, you must build your *blog strategy*.

OK, so you didn't know there was such a thing as blog strategy!

Well, assume that since you are learning internet marketing here, and you are not building a blog so your Aunt Minnie can see pictures of your wonderful kids.

That being said, let's think about whom you are building your marketing blog for.

Remember: Tinker to Evans to Chance.

Your marketing blog needs a direction. It cannot do it on its own.

So, contrary to what you might have heard or read, building a blog does not start with running over to wordpress.org and signing up for an account.

It starts here:

This is one of several tools that you will be using prior to launching your marketing blog. Now that is the 3rd time you have seen that phrase, because you should drill it into your head. You are not a blogger; leave that to the egomaniacs of the world. You are, plain and simple a

Marketing Blogger.

That is for you to know, not the general public. You see, you will become a Marketing Blogger that looks like any other information blogger.

Building a Marketing Blog is done in 3 steps:

- **Planning**
- **Preparing**
- **Optimizing**

The planning step begins with the Google Keyword planner as noted above.

It is free to set up an account, so let's get that done right now.

You will also need this account to access other Google tools.

While you are over at the Google spaces, make sure you sign up for Google + account.

When you create your profile, include your rel=author link in your bio.

This will become VERY important, as you will learn, when you set up your WordPress profiles.

Follow the instructions below to accomplish this. You should print this as a single page to walk you through these steps, while you are in your Google+ profile.

Linking your content to your Google profile is a two-step process. First, you add a link from your website or page to your Google profile. Second, you update your Google profile by adding a link back to your site.

1. **Link your content to your Google profile**
   Create a link to your Google profile from your webpage, like this:

   <a href="[profile_url]?rel=author">Google</a>

   Replace [profile_url] with your Google Profile URL, like this:

   <a href="https://plus.google.
   com/109412257237874861202?
   rel=author">Google</a>

   Your link must contain the? rel=author parameter. If it's missing, Google won't be able to associate your content with your Google profile.

2. Link to your content from your profile

The second step of the verification process is to add a reciprocal link back from your profile to the site(s) you just updated.

To add links to your Google profile: <u>Sign in to your Google profile</u>.

- Click **Edit profile**.
- Click the **Contributor to** section on the right (depending on how many photos you have, you may need to scroll to see this section), and then click **Add custom link**.
- If you want, change the visibility of your link, and then click **Save**.

To check your markup and see what author data Google can extract from your page, use the structured data testing tool. The tool only looks at a single page, so for now, you'll need to check author pages and content pages separately to see if they are linking to each other correctly.

Next...we want to discuss the keywords needed for your blog. Why do you need them, and how they will benefit you?

Ask yourself...

Is the keyword relevant to your website's content? Will searchers find what they are looking on your site when they search using these keywords? Will they be happy with what they find? Will this traffic result in financial rewards or other organizational goals?

If the answer to all of these questions is a clear "Yes!" proceed...

Search for the term or phrase in the major engines:

Understanding which websites already rank for your keyword gives you valuable insight into the competition, and also how hard it will be to rank for the given term.

Are there search advertisements running along the top and right-hand side of the organic results?

Typically, many search ads mean a high value keyword, and multiple search ads above the organic results often means "a highly lucrative and directly conversion-prone keyword".

Buy a sample campaign for the keyword at Google AdWords and/or Bing AdCenter

If your Marketing Blogsite doesn't rank for the keyword, you can nonetheless buy "test" traffic to see how well it converts.

In Google AdWords, choose "exact match" and point the traffic to the relevant page on your Marketing Blog.

Track impressions and conversion rate over the course of at least 2-300 clicks.

Using the data, you've collected, determine the exact value of each keyword.

For example, if your search ad generated 5,000 impressions, of which 100 visitors have come to your site and 3 have converted for total profit (not revenue!) of $300, then a single visitor for that keyword is worth $3 to your business.

Those 5,000 impressions in 24 hours could generate a click-through rate of between 18-36% with a #1 ranking which would mean 900-1800 visits per day, at $3 each, or between 1-2 million dollars per year. No wonder businesses love search marketing!

(see the Slingshot SEO study (http://bit.ly/1NsnYJe) for more on potential click-through rates).

Are you beginning to understand the 3 steps noted above?

When you do this correctly your test effectiveness will be reflected in the result:

Ok, now that is done we are going to start to use the Keyword Planner.

When you create your Marketing Blog, you need to create a keyword rich URL, and with your initial root domain (URL) you will being creating at least 5 sub-domains. This is accomplished with prefixes, and I will explain in detail shortly, all about this.

Your keyword research should look a little like the example below:

As you can see, my niche is Training Parrots.

This phrase gets about half the volume of "bird training" and "training a bird".

The reasoning behind this is that even if a person owns a parrot, unless they have owned parrots for years, to them it is first and foremost a bird.

So, as most people are inherently lazy, and they will just type in "bird training".

Keep this in mind when you do your keyword research.

Insight: look at the bottom 2 results. "training your bird" (400) and "train your bird" (1900)
Why did the last one get 5 more times the search than the one before it?

Because it is easier to type "train" than it is to type "training". (Go Figure).

Now that we have the keywords that we want to Market Blog for, so now we will secure my URL. After discovering (birdtraining.com) is taken, and not available, it is time to be creative.

So, based on the above analysis we would name our blog:

- birdtrainingmadeeasy.com as my root domain (URL)
- howtrainingabird.com (sub-domain)
- fastparrottraining.com (sub-domain)
- knowtrainingbirds.com (sub-domain)

So now we have the 4 top keyword searches under one domain. The prefixes in the subdomains will not count in SEO, because the actual Marketing Blog page will be optimized without the prefixes.

You are learning something very important here.

You may be wondering at this point how this all ties in to your marketing efforts. Well, the most obvious benefit is when you are a member of a community on Google +, every time you make a Marketing Blog post, it is automatically shared with all members of your community. The effect of putting your rel=author link in both your Marketing Blog and your Google+ accounts.

So, let's say you belong to 12 communities, and each community has 300 members, the math tells you that when you post on your blog, it goes to Google+ and 3,600 people see it.

Now, if you have been producing good, relevant content, and ask your communities, if they find it helpful, to share it with their communities, as well as Twitter and Facebook friends, you darn well know your information will flow. All the while as it circulates cyberspace, it keeps growing your **author rank**.

OK, so here is what is next:

Let's trot over to Namecheap.com and register our domains, our main URL only, not our sub-domains.

You can use whatever registrar you chose, but you should use Namecheap, simply because it is cheap and effective, no other reason, and it will be easier for you to follow any instructions, because there will be a lot of them.

Now after this step, which you will receive in our supplemental Box37A, we will be going over to HostGator to do our set-ups. Here you will not have a choice of hosting. The reasoning is enormous. Most of the larger hosting sites, like Go-Daddy, do not support word-press.org, or any other blogging platform for that matter. They also do not have a C-panel control, which is imperative in operating a Marketing Blog.

Not only are you going to learn how to fully set up your blog and fully optimize it, page by page. You will learn how to convert any existing website that you currently have, into a full Marketing Blog. This is a real "gem" because very few people know how to do this, in fact, very few people know that it can even be done.

Like the sign says, we better get going here, you have a lot of work to do. See you all on the other side of Box38......... all ready to go to make some money.

BOX 38

MAIN STREET USA

One in Forty-Six.

Welcome back. Hopefully you have enjoyed and learned from the previous three boxes, and, as promised at the end of Box 37, you will now get to see the purpose of becoming an affiliate marketer.

"Because it is the seed"

In several of the previous boxes you saw that IM has a very high failure rate.

Yes, you would be correct if you remembered 96%. Look at this pragmatically: The U in "Failure" could easily be U, and U alone.

It's time to avoid failure. It's time to take your IM affiliate marketing to the next level. Its time focus on what you have learned and bring it to where the real money and income resides:

Look at what businesses take out full page and half page ads. These ads cost between $800 and $1500 per month. These are your candidates. (Of course you can always look at the internet yellow pages).

While we are talking about yellow pages, keep in mind, that you will also be offering your clients, after you have you set them up on the internet, an up-sell to mobile marketing, which earns you lucrative **PPC** and **PPA** commissions. (You will learn that in Box39).

First let's start with YOU.

You will not get a second chance with the client!

What applies here is the old adage "First impression is the one they will stay with". You need to have your entire marketing plan structured before you begin off-line marketing.

Let's do a checklist. We have listed the bare minimum structure that you will need **PRIOR** to presenting your services to your potential client base.

- Your fully optimized web-site
- Email responder
- Full Blog site
- Your YouTube channel
- LinkedIn business page(s)
- Pinterest business page(s)
- Facebook business page(s)
- Website linked to Google Plus
- Well designed printed brochure
- Postcards- matching your brochure
- Business Cards matching postcards and brochures
- Register with your local **BBB**
- Business license/ DBA matching your business name

Keep in mind as you approach off-line marketing, most businesses that you approach, will have very little knowledge of what they need for on-line marketing of their business, but that does not mean they have very little knowledge.

They have the knowledge to be in business for themselves, and they are usually smart and resourceful people, and **they will make an instant judgment about your ability.**

When you make a professional and well prepared presentation, they will listen. You must be prepared for them to check you out on-line also.

Prosperity by Design

Invent yourself with one smooth flow throughout the entire web spectrum:

All your profiles must point to one single impression. And make damn sure all your profiles are complete and uniform. And make sure your profiles are complete and detailed. In this instance, more is better.

There is a lot of checking and rechecking to do in the list above, so I will give you a couple of days to get all your ducks in a row.

As Boxes 35-36-37 were all about Affiliate Marketing, this trilogy, Boxes 38-39-40 will all be on Main Street Marketing.

Our Main Street Marketing projects, will also be working in conjunction with our Affiliate Marketing.

Preview the following sequence before proceeding:

- Initial postcard mailing
- Follow up brochure mailing

- In person sales contact
- Email follow up
- Sales call (informational)
- Close the sale.

Box39 goes into detail for each one of these processes, along with selecting and marketing to a particular niche. Also, you will be learning the product creation packages, which will apply to various industry sectors.

This will outline, in detail, what has to be done, and where to get it done, for each package level.

The competition in the Main Street Marketing arena consists of the "canned" website sellers, that market their services to the professional trades. i.e. doctors, dentists, lawyers, accountants.

What they do is sell a canned website that blankets a single industry, then for free or little up-front cost, they sell it to the professional, and then charge them a monthly maintenance fee.
This is easy to counter because in most cases the professional never realizes that they do not own the site. They only own the URL. When the customization is completed, and it is populated by the professional and the office staff, all they have is a pretty brochure.

The professional then engages in the "canned" site seller on a monthly basis, and the $50.00-$100.00 monthly fee never goes away.

If the professional changes their mind, they are only left with his URL. The website and all the work that went into it is gone.

You just sell them the fact that what they buy from you, they will own forever.

So folks, we are burning daylight here, see you very soon in Box39.

P.S. At that top you noticed "One in Forty-Six". Only One in Forty-six internet marketers ever transition to Main Street Marketing.

This gives you one HUGE opportunity.

Rich and Marty

BOX 39

Main Street Marketing Systems

N ow, that you have progressed from Box38, you have all the requirements met.

IF NOT, then go back to Box38 and get your program in order.

Soon it will be clear to you that a worthwhile level of entry for a client you select will be 35 + 4. ($3500 initial payment +$400 monthly)

The reasoning is quite simple. At this pricing level you can earn enough to make a reasonable profit, salespeople can earn a living, affiliates can get paid, and your admins will be compensated, and there will still enough left on the table for you.

If you attempt to go below this level, unless there is great potential and a budget in view, it is simply not worth the time and effort.

Believe us, **the lower paying clients will suck the life out of you.**

When the level of potential earning is smaller and the stress level rises, this entire endeavor will cease to be fun. You will stop loving what you do; so you might as well go out and get a job. At least then it will be someone else's headache.

Educating your clients

This will be the key to all the UPSELL sales that flow from the client. When you provide a quantifiable service and your clients see the results, UPSELLS (the offering of additional and beneficial services) will occur.) Your clients see real benefit and you profit along the way!

The best way this is accomplished is to have face to face meeting with the client, after the work has begun. The personal contact you have with your client is important, as they start to see themselves with an internet presence.

This is where you can start to explain the width and scope of the project.

You are setting the stage for your expanded services.

First, let us look at the BASIC 35 + 4 program:

That is $3500.00 payment upfront paid to you to start the campaign project. Plus $400.00 per month for 6 months for the maintenance contract. We have several examples of client contracts on our main website and they are all effective, and free for you to copy and paste.

There are 2 reasons for a six-month contract:

1. It is a comfortable small commitment for most small business to pay.
2. When you show results at the end of the 6-month period, you can up-sell to the next level for a full 1 or 2-year contract.

WYSIWYG
(What you see is what you get).

- Initial Client Needs & Site Review
- Keyword Research
- Competition Review (3) to Identify Top Local Keywords and Opportunities
- Building a Hosted 5 to 20-Page Website
- Site Content Creation
- Recurring On-Page SEO of Top Pages
- Monthly SEO Ranking Reports
- Google Analytics Setup with Monthly Summary Reports.
- Initial page Conversion Rate Optimization Edits to Minimize Bounce Rate
- Social Media: Facebook and LinkedIn Social Profile Setup
- Google+ and Google+ Local (aka. Places) Page Setup Supporting Local Results
- Written and Distributed Press Release
- Call Tracking setup and tracking
- PPC Ad Management Setup for the SEO keyword phrases (on-going management optional)
- 404 Error Page Setup
- 4 to 6 Google Indexing Submissions (on topic).
- 1 or 2 Optimized, Original Articles
- Competitive Link Analysis Report
- E-mail Communication and Scheduled Consulting Call for Your Team Lead with admin Dedicated Client Liaison
- Business Listings Posted for Your Business Address
- HTML and XML Site-map Creation and Submission

Wow, you say, that seem like an awful lot of work for one client.

Well it certainly is not when:

We cannot overstate the importance of having all your systems organized; your clients will want to know what they can expect, and when they can expect it.

- You have two processes accomplished.
- You now have your sales sequence setup.
- You have your 35 + 4 delivery program setup.
- Now you have to systematize both of the processes.
- You have to segment the work.

Q. We know the salespeople will go out and sell the program. Who does what after a sales contract is dropped in your lap?

A. That is not the time to think about it. **NOW** in this present moment is the time. You will notice on the above 35 + 4 product package; several open doors have been set up.

Open doors in Social Media, open doors in email marketing, Blogs, PPC coupon campaigns, Landing pages, etc., etc.

They are All Up-Sells

So, the money never stops flowing from the client account, to you, and when the client sees progress from the campaigns, the money will continue to flow.

Trust management:

Social media has vast differences when compared to other advertising models. A SMM (social media marketing) professional understands that trust is about genuine interaction and relationship-building as opposed to just disseminating a message and giving a sales pitch.

Keep this in mind, you must deliver the concept of trust management to your client.

OK folks, we are starting to burn daylight here, on the other side of Box40; you will learn how to put all the systems together, and you will be given the tools you will need to make your system flow, from automated client billing to aggregating their profiles.

You will also learn how to set up your affiliate programs, so that the money you earn from a client keeps flowing long after the last time you see them.

So, continue to get your ducks in a row, and we will see you in Box 40.

Rich & Marty

BOX 40

Main Street Marketing

Generating the "Off-Line" cash flow.

Understand what you are selling

When you sit down with a prospective client the first time, don't make the bonehead mistake of selling the business owner SEO, Social Media Marketing, PPC, PPA, Google ranking, on-line visibility, video marketing, blogging, etc., etc.

<u>These are your tools, not theirs.</u>

A client **needs** to understand what your services will do for them.

YOU SELL 3 THINGS to your client:

CUSTOMERS– SALES– PROFITS.

This is what your perspective client needs to know about.

This will be the foundation of your marketing materials.

When you sit with your first client, which of the next 2 statements do you think will most likely capture his/her interest:

"I will get you one the first page of Google within 3 months" (maybe)

OR

Are you aware that 85% of people are searching for local business online?

Sadly, only 25% of small businesses actually show up on those searches, and if you're not one of them you're losing customers.

Don't talk to the client in industry terms that he may or may not fully comprehend.

As a business person he can certainly understand that more customers means more profits.

Successful businesses meet customer needs in ways that balance the cost of delivering satisfying results with the expenses that must be incurred to satisfy these needs. This also takes into account the prices that customers are willing to pay.

Segment your Markets

"Selling to everyone is selling to no one"

You will need to create a starting point for your Main Street Marketing campaigns.

Your ideal starting point would be in an industry that you have a base knowledge of. Or, at the very least, do as much research into the industry niche that you choose as your starting point.

Once you have selected the niche you will be marketing to, get yourself recognized as an expert in this niche. This will be accomplished by writing several articles related to the operation of this particular niche.

Let us use the Veterinary Industry as an **example**.

Just because you have owned a dog or cat does not make you an expert in this niche.

However, after doing your research, you write several articles titled "Building your Veterinary Business", "Attracting Clients to your Veterinary Business", etc., you soon become the recognized authority in this field.

You build your new Social Profiles targeted specifically to the Veterinary industry. Your aim will be to promote yourself **as the Leading Authority** on building and/or increasing a veterinary practice.

You create an Internet Marketing Blog on "Veterinary Business Building", populate it with genuine relevant information that is both useful and helpful to people in that industry, and you have created the basis on why they should and need do business with you.

It is all about creating the perception.

You are creating yourself as the #1 authority on website design and marketing for the veterinary industry.

When you select an industry that has such a far reach, the back-end possibilities are endless, because once you are established in your local marketing area, the entire world opens to you.

You will now become the **#1 leading authority** in veterinary practice building in New York (add your city here), to becoming the #1 authority in veterinary practice building in the USA.

You are learning something here that no other Main Street Marketers have learned to do.
All MSM's go out and attempt to sell their services to everyone and anyone who will listen to them. They are all competing for the same marketing dollar, to the same business people who have heard it all before. So, now it comes down to who will be the cheapest one to do the job.

There are a herd of them out there working Main Street and on the internet who will promise the world for $500 to a thousand bucks.

This is not what we do.

We are certified experts in a particular industry and we command top dollar for our services.

Actually, we are certified experts in many industries, because this is a true rinse and repeat process, niche by niche. When you approach a targeted prospect, and introduce yourself as a specialist that only works with veterinary practices, you have just captured their attention.

We have a friend in this market segment, who stated in his brochure, that his company is "**Approaching** 10 years working exclusively with veterinary practices".

Since he was only in this niche about 2 months, we applauded him for his use of a creative truth. You see, he only needed another 9 years and 10 months to actually "approach" his stated goal, but he was certainly approaching it.

None the less, it was a powerful headline.
This gives you instant authority and they will want to listen to what you have to say.

How to test your niche market?

Below is an example of a stock brochure that you can purchase from Staples.com500 brochures cost approx. $129.00 and 500 (8 x 10) large postcards for $69.95. Add industry specific business cards $49.00 or under 250 bucks you have entered the veterinary lead capture business.

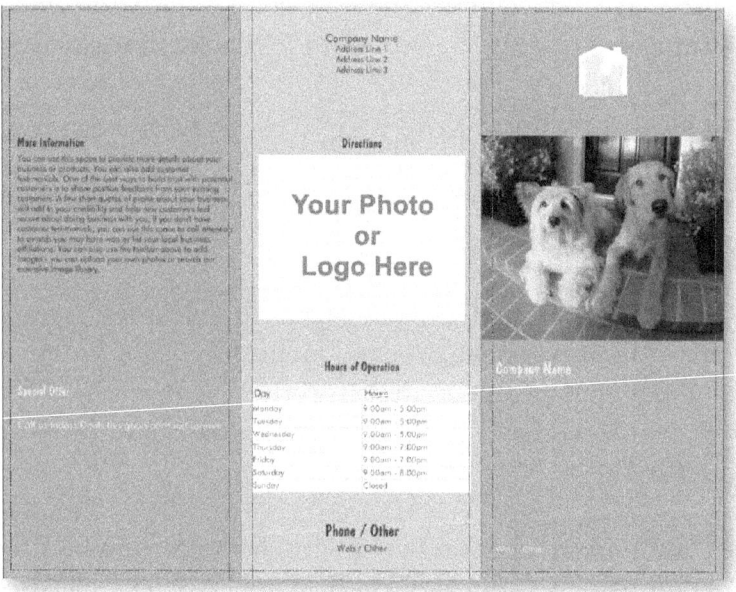

You mail the large postcard first, it will have very little impact, that is not the point. When you mail the brochure about 5-7 days later, they will start to recognize your name and logo. When your sales rep (affiliate) makes an in person sales call the prospect will at least be familiar with the brand.

Are YOU getting the message here......?

The marketing is about **THEM**, not about **YOU**, and they will understand this.

The above postcard, we borrowed from our friend. He used only one headline on the front of the card that said:

Did you see my pet?

When the recipient turned over the postcard to read, it simply stated:

"Of course you didn't, we did not know how to find you. Only YOU can solve the problem that is holding your business back."

Let's not go through all the creativity of someone else; let's just begin to convey some of messages that will have an impact on your market niche.

It is up to you to determine your own creativity. Once you start the process, you will be amazed at how easily it will flow for you. The main objective in starting the thought process is to emphasize FOCUS.

You need to focus on what is important and relevant to your target audience. The above examples show what is of interest to this particular market niche: Veterinarians.

Campaign Goals

Our initial goal would be for a 2% conversion rate, but for arguments sake say we only convert at 1%. (We would set a 4% conversion for ourselves).

So, our 1% conversion of 500 prospects, (5) buying our premium package of $3500.00, would result in a gross sale of $17,500.00. That is without any back end monthly service charges.

For our first campaign, we would be working in 10 industry niches, on a one week rotating basis, so at the end of 10 weeks, the yield would be $175,000.00. This still is not counting any back end monthly service agreements.

Assume that the service agreements standing alone is $300.00 as the monthly mean, when multiplying these 5 clients in each niche, there is a whopping $15,000.00 per month.

This keeps your back office admins happy and productive.

At this point let's construct our Blueprint for our Main Street Marketing.

- Select a URL that is industry specific for your niche.
- Create a Wordpress.org blog for your marketing site.
- Upload your landing pages to your blogsite.
- Create Gmail account with referenced Blog URL
- Set up your email sequence at AWeber.com
- Make directory listings of your URL.
- Create your Structured Data Markup within Google.
- Link your Blog-site to your Google Data Markup
- Open new Social Media Accounts with new URL reference
- Create article series at your distribution points.
- Guest post on niche related blogs.
- Prepare your brochures and postcards.
- Have your contracts ready.
- Establish your affiliate relations for niche specific products.

Now the list is to the point but it is by no means simple. Each step in the blueprint will have several sub-steps that need to be completed.

You will need to time budget about 1 week to get everything set-up. Once all your new socials are setup.... Share it Everywhere!!!!

The **secret dynamics** in Main Street Marketing is letting the client find you, not the other way around. Do not waste your time in cold calling prospects on the phone, it just doesn't work. You need to create the campaign that will spark the prospects attention. The prospects that show some interest from your brochures, or emails, will most likely Google your name or your company name, once that is done, the sale is almost done.

Keep in mind that you will be dealing with educated, savvy business people, so do not attempt to win them over with a lot of fluff.

One of the tools that we teach in our "Twenty Group" meetings is the use of **Google Scholar.** Here you will find "White Papers "on every industry and every niche of every industry was ever created in the last millennium. These reports will be the basis of populating a lot of your blog content. Especially if you know very little about that niche.

Use references and articles that pertain to the industry niche that you're marketing to at the time, to populate your blog. Those of you whom have never used Google Scholar, just go to www.scholar.google.com. You can thank me later for saving you countless hours in researching your niche. Well, the close of the day and we are burning daylight here, and you have a lot of work to do.

Since this is the last Box in this series, we invite you send your email in our opt-in box. You will receive a private email address that you can ask any questions you may have with issues in your business.

Thanks for reading, and the pleasure has been all ours.

Rich and Marty

ADDENDUM 1

WORDPRESS.ORG

This is the only place that you will call home for your Marketing Blogs.

Before we begin let us to clear up any confusion between WordPress.com and org.

WordPress.com uses the same core software, but focuses on the provision of free hosting services.

WordPress.org Overview:

WordPress.org is where "WordPress" the software is freely available to the public. Also for free are thousands of plugins, in addition to a number of "premium" plugins that can be purchased separately.

WordPress.org is terrific resource for "do it yourself" site owners. With support forums and tons of "how to" information, site owners can modify their designs and functionality to the limits of their creativity.

Also covered by the "ORG" side's documentation are the basics: installing WordPress, walkthroughs of your first posts and categories, etc.

With the WordPress.org Codex at your command, you'll be able to find everything you need to get WordPress (the software) rolling on your own domain.

Summarizing, with WordPress.org, the sky is the limit, and you won't need to pay to remove third-party ads.

With no restrictions, you can modify the core PHP, add fancy jQuery elements, use any theme you like, and/or install any plug-in you want. There's really only one thing missing... while one-click installation of WordPress.org often makes setup quick and easy, you will need a web host — and a host is not free.

Web hosting costs vary, but for "decent" WordPress hosting of a typical small- to medium-sized site, $7.00 to 20.00 per month is about the range.

You'll also pay about $10.00 for the annual renewal of your domain name.

WordPress.com Overview:

WordPress.com, things are flipped a bit. Installation is a snap, and the web hosting is provided free of charge. (please refer to Rich McKelvey's "second law of life", whenever you hear the term "free of charge").

The pros of no-cost hosting are clear. Aside from quality hosting services, you'll also get baked-in spam protection, automatic backups, automatic updates, proven security, and some WordPress.com plugins and services not found elsewhere.

The "cons" are that you cannot modify the PHP source code (even "newbies" often discover they want to make a few changes).

You can't upload any plug-ins, either — though there are plug-ins available on WordPress.com, these represent a fraction of the "21,000 and counting" available on WordPress.org.

Please do not kid yourself into thinking that we are going to give a list of all 21,000 plug-ins. However, on our site you will have a list of the top 100 plugins that you will need or ever want.

Finally, while you can choose among nearly 200 themes, you can't upload your own — and customization of these boilerplate themes is impossible.

Remember the asterisks? Most of them go away with a price tag. Here are some notable ones.
Your "domain name" will sound unprofessional, i.e. yourthirdchoiceofname.wordpress.com — though you can buy your own domain name, then map it to the WordPress.com system.

At a cost, of course, but one you'd also have with self-hosted WordPress.org

Don't like seeing third-party ads on your site? Which you have no control over, nor do you receive any income from, for $30-40/year, the ads can be removed.

A "custom design" package will let you get limited control over your chosen theme's design, such as changing the font and making basic CSS changes (no PHP, no FTP) — for $30/year.
Links advertising WordPress.com and themes cannot be removed.

Extra storage begins at $20/year.

If you want to roll-out your own videos, then Video Press is $60/year (note: YouTube embedding is available without the Video Press upgrade).

Premium themes have a price tag as well, ranging from about $45 to $200, each — and themes can't be transferred off WordPress.com if you later choose to go self-hosted. (that to me is like them stealing a $200.00 theme that you purchased).

While it was a recurring theme above, the cost should not be the primary factor in your decision, though it's always important to rec-ognize a simple truth, you get what you pay for — period. (Herein reinforcing Rich McKelvey's "second law of life").

Whether it's with managed WordPress hosting (this is the .org kind) or the (starts at) free WordPress.com hosting, at some point, you're going to pay to play.

While most self-hosted WordPress (the ORG kind) sites won't have the "nickel and dime" optional costs noted with the above WordPress.com.. "kill the ads" sorts of options, a year of "free" web hosting on WordPress.com — isn't going to save you much, if anything.

Self-hosting (org) tends to be only (slightly) more expensive, if not the same.

So if it's not the money, what should be the deciding factor?
Simple — it's you. This is your site, your brand, and your voice. The deciding point is how you wish to present yourself.

For certain types of blogging or personal sites, WordPress.com hosting offers an inexpensive method to share your thoughts, images, and connect with others.

Are you planning a private "our family" site?

For free, or near-free, you can probably ignore the clumsy "domain" name, the design limitations, and general "ad and link" clutter.

On the other hand, if you run a professional site. Your portfolio, an industry blog, a business Marketing Blog, then you are much more likely to want and need total control over your hosting, advertising, branding, and more.

You'll want to pick a great framework, as well as plugins that serve your needs. To make the most of your voice and brand, you'll also want to dive (or hire a pro to dive) directly into FTP, PHP, and all the other goodies that can bring your site bubbling to the top.

O.K . Now that you have knowledge about the differences, you now know more information than 98% of the bloggers out there today. **Statistic:** 95% of all blogs are abandoned within six months of starting.

ADDENDUM 2

CHEAT-SHEET CHECKLIST

Project Name: (Select offer to promote)

- Research keyword phrases – search volume
- Keyword Research
- Research keyword phrases – competition
- Competition Research Select 5-6 keyword phrases. Register domain name
- Add domain to hosting
- Set nameservers
- Brainstorm keywords & related words
- Create sub-domains
- Install WordPress on subdomains
- Download a WordPress theme
- Get Google Analytic Code
- Set blog settings, permalinks, reading, & discussion
- Activate Akismet plugin and enter API key
- Activate Theme
- Add Analytics code to footer
- Set sidebar (widgets) with Archives, Links, & Tag Cloud
- Edit blog About page
- Make blog post
- Link Your blog to your Google Authorship Page

- Ping blogs
- Bookmark blog posts
- (Clipmarks, Social Marker, Yahoo Bookmarks)
- Build out your Hubpages
- (Guestbook, Link List, Poll, RSS, Text modules)
- Link Hubpages to article
- Ping article
- Bookmark Hubpage posts & articles (Clipmarks, Social Marker, Yahoo Bookmarks)
- Build Wetpaint websites
- (Link to blog, offer, lens, article)
- Ping Wetpaint sites (Storyboard)
- Source images (640 x 480 pixels)
- Record voiceovers – Audacity
- Create music clips – Audacity
- Create title clips – Camtasia
- Assemble & add transitions – Camatasia
- Add audio & trim ends – Camtasia
- Synch title clips with audio – Camtasia
- Add callout text & other objects – Camtasia
- Produce as MP4 – Camtasia
- Create video info files
- Upload to YouTube
- Upload to Daily Motion